D1630095

ALBERT SPEER

ALBERT SPEER

CONVERSATIONS WITH HITLER'S ARCHITECT

JOACHIM FEST

TRANSLATED BY PATRICK CAMILLER

polity

First published in German in 2005 by Rowohlt as *Die unbeantwortbaren Fragen. Gespräche mit Albert Speer* and © Rowohlt Verlag GmbH, 2005

This English translation © Polity Press, 2007

Polity Press
65 Bridge Street
Cambridge CB2 1UR, UK

Polity Press
350 Main Street
Malden, MA 02148, USA

ISBN-10: 0-7456-3918-6
ISBN-13: 978-07456-3918-5

Typeset in 10.75 on 14 pt in Adobe Janson
by Servis Filmsetting Ltd, Manchester
Printed and bound in the United States by Maple-Vail

For further information on Polity, visit our website: www.polity.co.uk

CONTENTS

ILLUSTRATION ACKNOWLEDGEMENTS

akg-images: p. 12 (photo: Heinrich Hoffmann)
Bildarchiv preußischer Kulturbesitz: pp. 19, 21, 35 (photo: Heinrich Hoffmann), 73, 83, 95 (photo: Heinrich Hoffmann), 105, 114 (photo: Hanns Hubmann), 118 (photo: Hanns Hubmann), 131, 163
Bayerische Staatsbibliothek München: p. 49
ullstein bild: pp. 89, 146, 160, 166, 172, 193
Landesarchiv Berlin: p. 123

INTRODUCTION

The notes comprising this book refer to discussions that I had with Albert Speer after his release from Spandau prison. The editor of Ullstein Publishers, Wolf Jobst Siedler, had asked me whether I would be prepared to lend Speer a hand with his 'memoirs' by acting as an 'interrogating editor'. In fact, Siedler had contacted Speer during his years of imprisonment to secure the rights to the planned work, which – it soon became clear – already existed in a first draft. A number of other publishers, both in Germany and abroad, were also interested in the memoirs. But Siedler was awarded the contract.

In late 1966, at the urging of the American publisher Harcourt, Brace, Jovanovich, I was beginning to think of giving up my job as a senior television editor and writing the biography of Hitler that would appear a few years later. Siedler's request thus seemed to me both interesting in itself and useful for my own project. Speer was undoubtedly a prime witness, of the kind that historians seldom have at their disposal. Thanks to his special position of trust at Hitler's court, as well as his wide overall perspective and the critical detachment with which he had observed the final period of the Nazi regime, there was every reason to believe that he would reveal more about the personality of the dictator, and do so with greater accuracy, than any other participant had done. Furthermore, my previous portrait of Albert Speer in *Das Gesicht des Dritten Reichs*[1] had raised a number of questions to which I had been able to give only an approximate answer on the basis of the available sources, but which stood in need of greater elucidation. After brief reflection, I therefore agreed to the proposal.

Our work together began early in 1967. Despite evident reservations on both sides Speer proved an intelligent interlocutor, neither blinkered by prejudices (in so far as this lay in his power) nor grudging with information. With regard to Hitler's personality, he was the comparatively rich source I had expected, and in fact I immediately started to write down the many hints and suggestions that he offered me. To a greater or lesser extent, these were included in the body of notes that I was compiling for my planned biography. After a while, however, I also recorded more and more of Speer's general observations, without yet linking this to any clear purpose. They simply struck me as points of interest, in relation to the policies of the regime, the endless power struggles in the leadership, Speer's own position at the court, the type of disoriented defector that he perfectly embodied, and much else besides. The main things I eventually preserved were those which Speer, for whatever reason, omitted from his memoirs or included in a form that was either markedly different or, in a few cases, required further expansion.

To be sure, neither then nor in subsequent years did I contemplate writing a biography of Speer. Had this been in my mind, I would certainly have asked him further questions

concerning his personal development and his inner contradictions, motives and models, but instead I usually recorded
only what came up in the course of discussions that had no
particular aim other than putting together his books. I also
noted various arguments that inevitably arose between us
and Speer's reactions to many distressing issues – later also to
the success of his publications and the attacks he had to swal-
low, and finally the judgements that others passed on this
rather opaque man. Even then it seemed to me that Speer's
life, with all its self-deceptions, false emotions and moral
obduracy, was far more representative than he had ever realized, and that it significantly contributed to the picture of
German confusion that had made Hitler possible and perhaps almost unavoidable.

The rule that the manuscript should record only points
that Speer did not make in his published *Memoirs* does not
mean that some of his remarks do not correspond to events
that he described elsewhere. But it is never a case of merely
repeating the same thing. Often the reader will find supplementary factual or psychological detail that brings the historical picture to life and makes it easier to understand. This
is especially true in view of Speer's frequent refusal, despite
every encouragement, to include certain incidents in the
story of his life. It is still my view that his manuscript sometimes gives such a truncated account of things that it loses a
considerable part of its force as evidence. An example of this
is the tactical finessing with which he sometimes enforced
his demands as a minister, or – a closely related aspect – all
the considerations on the homoerotic character of his relationship with Hitler.

The notes record Speer's irritation when I actually asked
him about this one day. He was scarcely less annoyed at my
and Siedler's repeated attempts to elicit a detailed account of
his reckless, even 'deranged' visit to the Reich Chancellery

bunker on the night of 23–4 April 1945. Speer tried to justify his decision on the grounds that he had to take personal leave of Hitler. But such a farewell had already taken place three days earlier, after the celebration of Hitler's birthday. Were his feelings still so strong for Hitler and his inner circle – both of which Speer had for some time thought of as 'criminal' – that he would have 'despised himself for the rest of his life' if he had not made that quixotic gesture? Were they stronger even than his survival instinct, in a situation where he had to fear either a Soviet shell or a firing squad acting unceremoniously on Hitler's orders?

Years later, for whatever reasons, Speer again spoke to me of the gruesome last meeting with Hitler, marked by pathos as much as vulgarity, in an account that is more informative than the one in his *Memoirs* and assures the leave-taking of a place in history. Even then, he remained silent about his motives and about why he had for so long been unwilling to disclose what he felt on that occasion, which had evidently been locked away in some emotional closet; sometimes it occurred to me that he felt free to report on the events of that day only when they had been given a 'literary' closure through the publication of his memoirs. As a result, the considerably more extensive version contained in these notes conveys additional information about the peculiarities of Speer's character. This also applies to many other admissions on his part.

An all-embracing point of view was never recognizable in Speer's refusal to deal with one or another occurrence in his published memoirs. We may deduce from certain assertions or behaviour patterns that he was not at all – or anyway not generally – driven by the aim of diminishing his own guilt.

Mention should also be made of the ways in which we handled differences of opinion. If Speer, for whatever reason, did not want something to be recorded, we tried to explain to him its biographical importance. If he then continued to refuse, we usually refrained from trying to talk him round. After all, they were supposed to be *his* memoirs. In most cases, he limited himself to a bald 'I don't want to!' – which put an end to any attempt at persuasion. Only very seldom was it possible to change his mind.

A more serious conflict arose when Speer refused to address in his *Memoirs* the fact that the pogrom of 9 November 1938 had made no impression on him, for we considered that some account of his perceptions and feelings on that night was absolutely indispensable. Only after lengthy arguments, which once brought us close to breaking point, did he say that he was prepared to insert some consideration of the reasons why the outrage had left him so indifferent. Another case concerned his mother's highly critical report on a few days spent at the 'Berghof', which he perhaps arrogantly felt to have been unacceptable. After initial arguments he agreed to add an account of this in the *Spandauer Tagebücher*,[2] which he published a few years later, again with my assistance.

The reader should bear in mind that the objections raised by Siedler and myself reflect the state of knowledge in the late 1960s and early 1970s. But this limitation does not change much; few studies since then have gone any further. From time to time, an unsuccessful middle-aged historian by the name of Heinrich Schwendemann has drawn attention to himself by claiming finally to expose the lie of Speer's existence. Up to now, however, he has revealed little more than his own craving for recognition.

It is also necessary to explain that the following pages do not reproduce Speer's statements verbatim or in the exact order in which he made them, but rather constitute a condensed record. Only remarks or formulations in inverted commas should be regarded as actual quotations. Many statements contradict, or partly cut across, points made in his volumes of memoirs. But it was not my concern to compare the different versions or to make them tally with one another. In the end, inconsistencies were part of Speer's nature. I composed most of the notes in the evening, straight after work sessions typically spread over three or four days. We would usually meet at Speer's home in Heidelberg, but often we changed the rendezvous to the Schloss Korb hotel near Merano or to the island of Sylt. Over time I acquired a kind of 'interpreter's memory', which enabled me to retain for a time quite long explanations as well as the linguistic peculiarities of an interlocutor who repeatedly took things back or strayed from the point.

It should also be pointed out that Speer spoke extremely hesitantly, and whenever it was a question of personal or emotional matters he was tentative or even awkward with words. At times it was as if it was not a thought but control of a thought which dictated what he said. Nearly always he seemed to be weighing things up, with repeated pauses, rather than expressing himself briefly and emphatically. This was all the more striking because for many years he had been the economic dictator of Europe. More than once I asked myself whether the man opposite me really was the genuine Speer.

The same question had been on the lips of the British sergeant who, in late May 1945, hurried up the great staircase of Schloss Glücksburg, past the many unknown faces of the castle staff, to arrest the minister: 'Who is Speer?' I kept wondering whether the twenty or more years of imprisonment had broken him inside and, as it were, altered his personality. Or had the personality change taken place in the previous period, when he bestrode the lonely commanding heights and, thanks to Hitler's trust in him, was capable of imposing nearly anything he thought appropriate? As regards his faltering speech, we may also ask whether its roots lay in the largely unthinking existence he had led for such a long time. Perhaps the questions thrown up by his life had virtually never entered his consciousness – or at least only when he had had to face the Allied interrogators, the Nuremberg court and the countless people demanding information of him.

Finally, it should be mentioned that these notes did not originally follow the chronology of Speer's life, but reflected the vagaries of our conversation; I have given them a certain temporal order only for the purposes of this book, without being able to avoid altogether the occasional forward or backward reference. Whenever my 1999 biography of Speer spoke of an 'editor's note',[3] it had in mind the notes that are presented here. Overlapping with the biography has been avoided as much as possible, and besides many of Speer's statements appear here in a changed or even novel light. The end product may be of interest to a wide readership, as it concerns a man who counts as a key figure in the Hitler years less for his own position of power than because of his troubled personality.

The notes stand in their own right: that is, they assume only a sketchy, not precise or detailed, knowledge of Albert Speer's life. They do not change the picture in its essentials. But they do significantly supplement and deepen it, and they allow others to have a say in elaborating the more general framework. They also set in sharper relief a number of questions that later generations ask themselves about this highly typical figure from the age of totalitarianism. Nevertheless, in order to read these notes most accurately, it will be useful to know something about Speer's origin, trajectory or major companions and about the Hitler regime itself.

Many of Speer's statements that appear in these notes could not be included in my biography, because they would have digressed too much or otherwise impaired the dramatic sweep that any literary account requires. For a while I was even unsure whether to publish them at all, especially as, after the appearance of the Speer book, my main idea was to hand the bundle of notes over to an institute. But, when I again looked through what remained after the passages I had previously used, it seemed to contain a sufficient amount of informative material, whose publication would certainly make more sense than to let the pages fade on the shelves of some archive, as often happens in the academic world. Along with many discrete touches, one long note among my papers tipped the scales. Gitta Sereny's thick volume on Speer argued that, in his farewell visit to the deep bunker in the Berlin Chancellery, he had in no way expressed his defiance of Hitler's order for destruction, and that he had merely been putting on an act when he had claimed otherwise; Speer was never the hero he made himself out to be. I had already cast doubt on this objection in my biography of Speer, thanks to the account of his leave-taking from Hitler that I had elicited from him. But inevitably I had left out of consideration many of the exceptionally significant details that he mentioned to me. They certainly told an attentive reader that Speer was no 'hero' – and to this extent I could agree with Gitta Sereny. In fact, he was something much more disturbing: a narrow-minded idealist, who offered his services to any superior force. Right to the end, Speer felt obliged to show personal loyalty to the destroyer of his own country, a man he perceived as a criminal. It was a key scene, which the notes in my possession described for the first time with a wealth of detail. It uncovered a 'German abyss', as I put it at the time to Siedler. And scarcely ever did I feel so opposed to Albert Speer, or find so revolting the world in which he had lived, as when he advanced explanations for his course of action. His readiness to maintain certain conventions, even in relation to a mass murderer, brought out the desperate inferiority of the many figures of Speer's ilk. It threw light on one of the conditions that had led to Hitler and ultimately made it impossible to get rid of him.

The leave-taking in the bunker, like a number of other events, points to the general theme to which my conversations with Speer and the ensuing notes constantly return: that is, the enigma of his life. Speer became so hopelessly caught up in the contradictions which accompanied and eventually ruled his life that, as time went by, he increasingly lacked even a half-convincing answer to them. In the end, he himself became the greatest enigma. The present notes, rather disorderly and erratic as they are, perhaps make this process more vivid than the finished text of biography is able to do.

The question as to what Speer knew about the genocidal crimes of the Third Reich, which has overshadowed the constant debate about his personality, is never to the fore in these notes. In any event, he knew quite enough to feel abhorrence for the creatures of the regime with whom he became entangled, beginning with the persecution of political opponents immediately after the Nazi seizure of power, and continuing through the countless illegalities and the tormenting of religious or racial minorities up to the deliberate unleashing of war. I have always found much more unsettling the thought that a man from his social and family background, having the moral standards with which he was brought up, could be so blindly captivated by a vicious regime boastful of its own barbarism. Speer's often biting displays of contempt for top Nazis to his left or right do not make things any better but add to the irritation that an observer feels.

These very facts raise the question of questions handed down by the various rulers of that time, which until now has remained without even a partly adequate answer. What precautions might provide some security against such a loss of all standards? And – perhaps a source of even greater concern – do any such precautions exist at all?

DRAWING CLOSER

January 1967. With Speer and Siedler on Sylt. Speer visited me a few weeks ago. When I saw him walking somewhat jerkily up the garden path with a battered briefcase in his hand, it triggered for a moment the doubts that had first appeared at the thought of beginning a kind of 'interrogating collaboration' with Hitler's 'friend'.

Our conversation was less of a problem than I had expected. Speer struck me as cultivated as well as completely lacking in emotion. The mechanical coldness in everything he says about the past is confusing, but it is disguised or made less conspicuous by his unsure and faltering manner of speech. Agreement: I'll first read the presently half-finished manuscript, on the basis of the Spandau draft and the later notes; he thinks that all in all it comes to around two thousand pages. Then the first editorial discussion.

Speer again very charming. Already in Spandau he read the portrait in *The Face of the Third Reich*, and he now realizes that, in that book and the various accounts by the British historian Trevor-Roper, he learned something about the period and his own role, whereas nearly everything else has been irrelevant. But he would not say what he learned about himself there. Maybe later, he said. Still a sense of holding back, and now and then little signs of mistrust on both sides. It was as if we were sizing each other up.

After eating, a walk on the mudflats. Speer did not seem surprised when – after a few questions about Spandau, the generals, his then young, now so successful colleagues and, of course, Hitler – we came to what he had known about the crimes of the regime and how he had reacted to at least the suspicion that must have come over him. I had prepared for our talk by acting out a 'cross-examination' with Siedler, in which we reviewed his known excuses and others that we thought he might make. Siedler's view is that this will (and should) be one of the central themes of the *Memoirs*.

But Speer had answers to everything, and it cannot even be said that they were implausible. Later, Siedler said that Speer had had twenty years to prepare them, whereas we had given ourselves only a couple of hours. We agreed that he did not seem insincere – more melancholic. For example: 'What's the point of all these journalist's questions?' After all, I chipped in, at Nuremberg he stood up to questioning by Justice Jackson and the other prosecutors, so now he is naturally doing the same with us. Siedler retorted that at least one aspect made us laymen better questioners than the prosecution at the Nuremberg military tribunal: we had Speer's trust. Do we have it? Perhaps less than Siedler thinks. But there is one thing in our favour: this time, unlike in Nuremberg, it is not a matter of life and death.

Addendum next morning. So, I said to Siedler, how Speer sees himself or would like his image to pass down to posterity is perhaps again a matter of life and death for him.

Albert Speer and Adolf Hitler, May 1943

▬▬ Further discussions. This time about architecture, the Capital of the World and Hitler's share in planning it. Everything still very tentative and reserved. Attempt to gain an initial overview. Siedler spoke in detail about his uncle, who in the late 1920s had designed the building at the old Reich Chancellery and was naturally known to Speer. This connection, Speer said, had played a role in his decision in favour of Propyläen Verlag.[1] Next about the architects Behrens, Taut and Poelzig. And finally about his teacher Tessenow, of whom he still thinks with warm admiration. In Speer's view, his simplicity would not be wasted again today. Then about the winding up of the great plans, which began with the war and which Hitler reluctantly accepted.

Again the vigilant look on his face as soon as we came to political matters. In the evening I commented to Siedler that, in everything Speer says, he seems to be asking what is at stake. 'He must have learned that in forty years – on pain of being eaten alive.' Siedler thought I was mistaken. Anyway he could see nothing like that in Speer's behaviour; rather, he was amazed by his lack of inhibition. But he admitted that considerable reservations were still visible.

===== Speer complains that after 1945 he was not able to speak with his parents. An impression that they were the only people he felt a real need to justify himself to. He said that he often dreamed of them, and it was always a question of trying to get them to understand him. He would have liked to explain why their world had meant so little to him at the time. 'I was a kind of *Wandervogel*,[2] he said, 'though in my own introverted way: that is, without songs and camp fires.' He had been at home in a kind of counterworld.

Siedler then asked whether he had wanted from his parents only the recognition that they owed him (as the black sheep among the three sons) and had never actually expressed. His father had even flatly denied him recognition as an architect. We both had the impression that he had never fully recovered from that, and that in the end he had

still wanted them to be proud of him: as a great architect, a
great minister and a great defendant.

===== We called this Speer's most salient experience: that all
his life he had been 'everybody's darling',[3] for his teacher
Heinrich Tessenow, for Hitler, for the Nuremberg judges, for
the guards at Spandau, and wherever else. But evidently not
for his parents, whose coldness still visibly troubles him late in
life. In a way he is even now a kind of 'darling'. This opened
up huge opportunities to him, which he knew how to exploit.
But it was also the problem of his life, even his undoing.

===== Speer on Goebbels: he was sly, base, cold and insen-
sitive, power-conscious. Nothing but repulsive features. But
they added up to a personality that had not failed to impress
him, however much he had abhorred every detail. After a
brief pause he asked naïvely: 'Is that possible?'

===== March 1967, Heidelberg. Work on the manuscript.
Despite some particular difficulties, my proposed system of
symbols for the shortening of the two to three thousand
pages of his manuscript is proving its worth. He handles
things with a great, almost professional circumspection, and
grasps what I mean even before I have given my reasons for
shortening or expanding a passage in the text.
    On Hitler. Cannot get away from him. Still a kind of 'cen-
tral star' of his existence. Scarcely any noticeably sentimental
tone in many of the things he says about him as a person –
or, more accurately, as a client and lover of architecture.

===== Speer reports that, by 1938 at the latest, Hitler was
displaying an intense fear of time; he would not grow old,
he had said 'in nearly every conversation' for a certain
period. The peculiarly obsessive side of his being. At

that time Hitler was prey to a strange disquiet, in sharp contrast to the seeming casualness of the early years of their acquaintance.

Speer said that, soon after the annexation of Austria, Hitler had told him in conversation that he wanted to be buried in a sarcophagus on the roof of a bell-tower planned for the city of Linz, if possible alongside his mother. Speer still seemed to find this moving and for a moment was disturbed by my interjection about 'Valkyrie cliffs as skyscrapers'. He also thinks that Hitler's direct flight into aggression goes back to that fear of time.

My objections did not disabuse him. Awe? Sentimentality? Fear of betrayal? Something is still glowing in the great heap of ashes.

===== At Siedler's in Berlin. Initial opinion about Speer. In agreement with Siedler that he is practically minded, sober, managerial. At the same time, 'German' in a limitlessly old-fashioned way: i.e., idealistic, romantic, as well as a little vaporous. Feeling only as a 'feeling for nature'. What did he feel listening to Bach or Beethoven that supposedly meant so much to him? Today he gave an awkward answer to my question and used words like 'beautiful', 'expressive' and 'heart-stirring'. Altogether, a mixture of real incompatibles. Is that too perhaps 'German'?

===== As if trying to wrong-foot us, Speer spoke today of the Webers in Heidelberg, the successful and highly regarded cabinetmaker, and of how his affection for their daughter 'Gretel' developed. At first it was only a schoolboy's fantasy, 'the usual stuff', as he added with uncharacteristic informality. Then they got together more and more often, on the basis of their shared fondness for theatre, literature, music and especially nature.

But, he said later, at least as important had been the warmth and kindness of the girl's parents, whose home was far more spontaneous, less rigid and ceremonial than that of his own parents. Everything else then 'happened by itself'. He had been re-reading some letters from that time and found 'the purest idea of something like platonic love'. But he did not want to make a laughing-stock of himself: 'Those were the most wonderful days.' And even today he has feelings of deep gratitude towards the Webers. The marriage took some more years. They married on 28 August and were proud when Gretel's father immediately discovered that it was the anniversary of Goethe's birth.

Siedler and I agree that these somewhat tangential but very personal remarks indicate a turning point in our relationship with Speer, and that perhaps he will now have the trust in us that we need for our work.

====== The evening with Siedler discussing the type of 'idealistic' German that the Speer of the 1930s visibly embodied in great measure. We were agreed about its engaging aspects in personal intercourse. But the picture immediately changes when this type appears in public life and perhaps acquires influence and power; then the inclination to set the world to rights comes to light, along with the 'absolute', one might also say ruthless, side of the personality. It is significant that Speer clearly belonged to Hitler's radical entourage. Siedler notes that, as he suspected, Speer had at all times been willing to ride over hedge and ditch. And over other things too, I added. We made it one of our tasks to encourage Speer to draw a self-portrait of this type.

====== Speer mentions how reassuring and confidence-boosting it was that Hitler never asked about his membership of the NSDAP or pushed him to join the Party. He says:

'I concluded that I was allowed to be apolitical, and I immediately drew the further fallacious conclusion that everyone
was allowed to be.'

Despite this insight, Speer still holds to the view that in
the 1930s Hitler had a side to him that was both confident
and generous. We argued about this. I pointed out that, if
Hitler never asked about his Party membership, it may have
been because he had long ago obtained the answer from
others. Besides, Speer's membership might have been a
matter of indifference to Hitler, if – and this could not have
escaped his notice – Speer had been 'blindly' attached to
Hitler, as he put it somewhere in the manuscript.

That evening Siedler and I spoke about the astonishing
weakness of Speer's thinking when it came to judging Hitler.

━━━ April 1967. Improvements in the editing system and
initial verdict on the newly arranged opening chapter. Much
of it still too diffuse, and I advise Speer to make the necessary cuts himself. In everything practical, he is still perfectly
sensible and creates no problems. A few differences of judgement. Sometimes an impression that he agrees with my proposal almost a little too readily.

━━━ Discussion of Karl Otto Saur, who took over Speer's
post in April 1945. Highly disparaging judgement, something almost like excitement in his otherwise composed
voice. Quite unusual. Perhaps for this reason some surprise
in Siedler and myself. Speer's basic reproach is that he
behaved in exactly the same way as himself, only two years
later: obedient to Hitler and submissive. Obviously sensing
the discordant impression that this makes on us, he tones
down the judgement, not without embarrassment. But it
remains contemptuous. 'The kind of courtier type who
throws himself at you', he says. People working under his

predecessor as armaments chief, Fritz Todt, called Saur 'Todt's booming newsreel'.

===== Speer says that morally he was always completely sure of himself. But perhaps that became his undoing. The distillation of his experiences, so to speak, was that you have to be deeply distrustful of yourself and especially of intense feelings. Anyone incapable of that will sooner or later come unstuck, under certain political conditions.

===== Speer said this evening that, having been over-whelmed by Hitler's appearance in the Hasenheide in the early 1930s,[4] he passed through a stage in which he looked to collect himself and to gain a certain distance. It is true that he became a Party member, but there were periods of critical detachment, and in the following months he more than once asked himself whether he had not become too involved in politics. But these were only passing moods.

Hitler got to know him during the work on the Reich Chancellery immediately after the seizure of power, and it did not take long for Speer to be won over by him: by his little gifts, his charm, and the glances in which astonishment and visible appreciation could be felt. He was naturally flattered, but there was no more to it than that. Occasionally he even joked about the signs of preferential treatment that his entourage, as always, pretended to detect more clearly than he did himself.

Speer ended his episode-rich account by saying that he really succumbed to Hitler only when he held out the prospect of a leading role in the reshaping of German cities, especially Berlin. Or anyway he then came close to surrendering. He was finally lost when Hitler placed a whole world at his feet, by telling his wife soon after they were introduced in 1934: 'Your husband will be given contracts and opportunities such as no architect has had in living memory.'

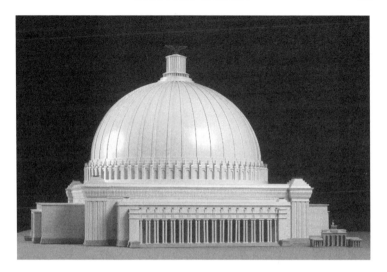

Speer's model for the Grosse Halle, to be built in the World Capital 'Germania'. The building, with room for 180,000 visitors, would have been the largest in the world. Beside it on the right, for purposes of comparison, is a model of the Brandenburg Gate.

Returning to a theme we had discussed before, he said that he had sometimes had doubts about his artistic temperament, especially as he had chosen the profession of architect more or less for the sake of his father. But then he became an artist in such a degree that all his wavering ended. 'From then on I was no longer unsure', Speer continued. 'And I'd like to know which ambitious young man still under thirty would not have taken seriously such a mark of favour from the most powerful man in the country. A world at my feet . . . Who would not have felt dizzy at the thought! It was not long before I was head over heels in love with Hitler.'

═════ Heidelberg. Speer took from a cupboard one of the cards that Hitler entrusted to him when they were discussing plans for Berlin. One side shows a design for the Grosse

Halle, the other for a triumphal arch. Both sketches date from the time of the Landsberg imprisonment or the months immediately after it.[5] 'Make that!' Hitler said when the ideas for rebuilding Berlin took more definite shape.

The drawings make it clear how early Hitler formed his ideas. He was planning triumphal arches at a time when he was a failed provincial politician serving a jail sentence. His amazing power to deny reality. But the sketches also confirm Speer's view that Hitler lacked one major requirement to become an important architect: he was incapable of questioning an idea he had come up with and considering alternatives.

Speer largely stuck to Hitler's guidelines – as he admitted – and made serious changes only in relation to the Grosse Halle. In return, he 'almost slavishly' followed Hitler's proposed measurements for it. The sketch showed, on the steps of the Halle, some vanishing-points that represented people really vanishing as tiny figures in front of the monstrous building. Speer prepared a huge blow-up of the drawing, calculated the proportion between the human points and the façade, and thus discovered Hitler's conception of magnitude. Then he complied with it. Nevertheless, he says that Hitler treated him as an equal in architectural matters and often gave way to him. But it was Speer who gave way over the Grosse Halle, I objected; that was his real 'planning sin', together with the destruction of the centre of Berlin. Had he often thought in those days of Tessenow's simplicity? He raised his shoulders in apparent perplexity: 'I was caught up in a completely different world.'

===== Speer on the World Capital 'Germania' that he planned together with Hitler. He was on a high in those days, and even now, looking back, he 'feels as if he is

These too were built by Albert Speer: the domes of light at the 1937 Reich Party congress in Nuremberg, during a speech by Adolf Hitler.

standing on air'. Perhaps this explains why, if not the town-planning solution, then the Grosse Strasse and everything connected with it, the whole architectonic concept in the narrow sense of the term, was such a terrible failure. For all things great, someone once said, you have to be cold even in your heart. That was not the case either for him or for those who worked with him. This ecstatic freedom, as well as the inexhaustible funds, made them forget all measure. Each and every one of them lost a sense of limits.

And yet, Speer corrected himself later, some of the constructions still appear to him successful. Besides, he would not want to have missed a single day from those times. When else has an architect had the opportunity to create a *Gesamtkunstwerk*? 'At least I had the opportunity, even if the work never came to fruition.'

===== Further to our discussion of the plans for 'Germania', I received from Speer a handwritten note in which he said:

> It may be of interest for the study of Hitler's early years that my list of his sketches contains the following written notes:

122	Berlin	Great Hall	circa 1924
123	Berlin	South Station	circa 1924
124	Berlin	State Library	circa 1924
125	Berlin	Great Arch	circa 1924

These notes were made by my former office manager Otto Apel. The 'circa' indicates that Hitler did not express himself precisely about the year of origin. Of course, attempts were made at the time to attribute this conception to him *at the earliest possible date* [Speer's emphasis]. But, as Hitler told me in summer 1936 that 'I did these drawings ten years ago', a later date is probable.

He did not come back to the idea of a new state library: it did not feature in the catalogue of emblematic buildings to be constructed on Neue Strasse. But it is possible roughly to calculate the proportions that Hitler intended for the library from the scale figures of people in the sketch – they are approximately one-third of a millimetre high. The building (at 14 mm high and 65 mm wide) would have been 70 metres in length and 460 metres in height. The main part (17 mm high) would have had an approximate height of 85 metres, on which a statue (with Pallas Athene) would have stood 25 metres high. Hitler wrote by hand on the sketch: 'State library'. On the reverse of the sheet are evidently a number of variants for this state library. Hitler did not come back to his plan for the South Station after he had accepted my sketches.

===== A kind of additional snippet. Hitler evidently found it relatively easy to give up the new state library, because he had another building as a substitute. Anyway, he said on occasion that the burned-out Reichstag should be rebuilt and used as a state library; after all, Paul Wallot's construction was architecturally 'very respectable'.

===== Speer on Hitler's tendency to have a say about everything, to express his views most emphatically on every question, even when he lacked the necessary expertise. This, Speer now knows, made him little different from a 'bar-room politician'. But Speer himself was so apolitical that he did not even know what bar-room politics was like, and so he admired Hitler's freedom of mind and self-assured judgements. He called him a 'highly gifted amateur'. Later, Speer somewhat revised his view of Hitler the architect: he had to add that Hitler often 'got it right' at the first attempt. He drew for us from memory the sketch of a column by his rival Hermann Giesler and then inserted the corrections that Hitler spontaneously made. They were indisputably an improvement.

2

IN THE INNERMOST CIRCLE

May 1967. Speer recalled that in 1935, when he acquired his 'work cabin' in the Alps, his wish had been not so much to remain at all times in close reach of Hitler as to escape the unpredictable moods to which he was exposed in Berlin. For him it was the usual question of a place for quiet work, but the 'hectic Hitler' did not permit him to have it.

But presumably – he added later – he had also wanted his residence to be not too far from Hitler's. Who can remember what one's motives were so long ago? In any case, he didn't think twice when a couple of years later Hitler offered him a house in the Obersalzberg area. And, of course, he had felt that he was being singled out for special honour.

══════ On the days in Obersalzberg, which he describes as so terribly dreary. How did he bear it? Speer referred to his theory that different 'circles', unconnected with one another, were preoccupied with themselves and their own striving for power. I retorted that one could understand that, but not what he had been doing. He offered to expand the passage in the manuscript where this is treated in a single sentence. He was more embarrassed when I added that the Berghof[1] had, as it were, risen above and cancelled out the 'circles'. He seemed at a loss: 'You couldn't avoid it', he said finally. 'It was just that – the Führer's circle.' Today he sometimes thinks (and perhaps already thought then) that someone who rose as high as he did, and who wanted to rise even higher, also had to put up with the baser things in life.

Speer seemed confused when I remained sceptical. 'Believe me', he said, 'I had nothing in common with Schaub, Brückner and Morell.[2] Who could have been more alien to me?' – Precisely.

===== I said it struck me that he had considered himself aloof from the wielders of power in the regime but not from their politics. Not a word had been said about that. He found it a pertinent objection and said that he would insert a few episodes or reflections in connection with it.

===== Hitler liked to fantasize about himself in previous centuries. Often he showed astonishing knowledge of them, said Speer. During the Russian campaign he once remarked that the German emperors had also been major founders of cities; he had always seen that as their most impressive cultural role, although it was not very well known. Just as they spread a network of towns and palaces across the land, it was necessary to keep this up in the East. With an eye to Himmler, he added that we should not so much honour the emperors as learn from them.

===== Hitler especially liked to speak of the revival in the arts that would occur, or was already occurring, under his rule. He mentioned Periclean Athens and Lorenzo's

Florence as exceptional predecessors. But one day there would be talk of a third great cultural centre in history. Another time he spoke of the autobahns as his 'Parthenon' and said it was his ambition to go down in history as a kind of 'kinsman' of Pericles.

In this connection, he boasted in 1938 that he had brought about 'great improvements' in painting and sculpture within the space of a few years, through the annual German Art Exhibition. As a member of the jury he could see better than anyone how things were progressing. 'The dilettantes are scared or stay away.' That's how it should be, he added. Speer also said he still believed that Hitler had wanted to go down in history more as a patron of the arts than as a military commander. War, as Hitler saw it, had been a necessity – or his 'accursed duty', as he often put it in the latter years – whereas the arts corresponded to his deeper inclination. A long argument about this. Later, with Siedler, about Speer's incapacity for psychological insights, in this case relating to something almost completely obvious.

===== Hitler had taken the view that great art is always but a reflection of the political grandeur of a people and its leadership. When he spoke of the 'blossoming of art' that had begun through him, he always thought that his rule and everything that came with it would thereby experience something like a justification. In art and artworks he was ultimately celebrating himself alone.

===== Hitler especially liked the art of the Italian Renaissance and mannerism, Titian, Palma, Guido Reni and so on. The new Reich Chancellery and the rebuilt Berghof already contained pictures mainly from that time; his private favourites Grützner, Makart, Spitweg or Achenbach he evidently did not consider representative enough. He had a special fondness for a semi-nude by Bordone, a member of the Titian school, and a colour sketch by Tiepolo that hung in the large living-room at the Berghof.

Hitler could not relate to German artists from the same period: he found Dürer and the artists of the Danube school, for all their 'charm' (as he often put it), too 'provincial' and pedantically 'German'. Of Cranach's numerous pictures of Venus and Eve, he once said that they were 'unaesthetic' and mere 'figures of art'; 'no woman in the world looked like that'. Anyway, those 'pole-like bodies' meant nothing to him.

===== Heidelberg. Speer out attending to a few things. I took the opportunity to have a few words with Frau Speer. In recent weeks she has been visibly keeping her distance, and when that has not been possible her expression at meal-time has been absent or even aloof. This time too, as soon as the conversation drew close to the book project, she showed an almost anxious evasiveness. When I made the third refer-ence to the manuscript, she most noticeably fell silent for the third time. I then avoided any further allusion to it. Obvi-ously she finds the whole business deeply unpleasant. When Speer arrived and immediately began to talk about our work, she left the room without a word.

===== In the spring of 1939, Hitler sometimes said that he really needed two lifetimes to achieve what 'destiny' had charged him with; yet he had not been granted even one. When he noticed the doubt on Speer's face, he added that the doctors had not said as much but that he knew it.

===== Hamburg, June 1967. Today Speer came with Frau Kempf, his secretary and close friend of many years. Conge-nial, quiet and decisive. Not uncritical towards Speer, as one could tell from a few (obviously most discreet) remarks that she made. A very independent person. When asked, Speer said that she had energetically contradicted him even when he had been a minister, but never in the presence of others.

At first about the Nuremberg trial and her role in obtaining the documents needed for Speer's defence – a role she had taken on without having been asked. All this from Kransberg, where she was kept in a loose kind of internment, and where the British authorities had no idea what she was doing. She spoke of the adventures she had had to go through in those months as a document-smuggler, but she did not put on any airs. 'I just had to get on with it.'

At some point we again touched on what people in Speer's circle had known about the crimes of the regime. Initial impression that Frau Kempf was carefully considering her words, as she did not want to say anything that would give herself or Speer away. Then a sense that this was her style. I believed her that she had heard nothing about the mass murders, not even oblique references.

She mentioned one of the drivers at the ministry, who confessed to her after the war that he had heard at the time about what was happening in the camps. Only rumours, of course, and the man had added that even so he would not have believed the whole truth – or what everyone today can read about them. It would simply not have been 'credible'.

When she asked the driver why he had never said a word to her about it, he looked at her in bewilderment. How could he, a mere lance-corporal, have dared mention it to her and therefore, through her, to the Führer's powerful and trusted minister? Besides, he would have had to name names, precise incidents, and so on. He had had a high opinion of his minister. But he could not have been sure of how he would have reacted. Presumably Herr Speer would even have been compelled to make an official report, and that would have landed him in terrible trouble. Only a naïve person could reproach him.

Frau Kempf thought the man was quite right. Presumably she too would not have believed anyone who had reported the mass murders to her. 'Who could think that was true?' she added. And: 'Did the Allies believe it, who certainly had reports from their secret services and were much more suspicious than we were?' In any event, they had not drawn the obvious conclusion and had not acquainted the world with the facts.

===== Frau Kempf also said she had often had the impression that, while Speer's leading colleagues, Hettlage, Brugmann, Kehrl and others, certainly hailed the minister's political ambition, they also almost imperceptibly sneered at it. They evidently could not imagine that Hitler had been serious when he had once or twice hinted that Speer would be his successor. In their view, the political loner Speer would not have got very far against the phalanx of Goering, Goebbels and Bormann. Not to speak of Himmler.

Speer contradicted her by saying that he had not been without prospects in the succession debate. I pointed out that his whole position of power rested on Hitler's trust, and that Hitler would no longer have been there when it came to the question of a successor. Speer looked silently in front of him and shook his head, with the smile of someone who knows better.

===== I told Speer and Frau Kempf of the BBC radio broadcast that my father listened to at Christmas 1942. After the war, he said that he had first regarded as Allied war propaganda the claim that tens of thousands were being 'mechanically' slaughtered in the East – rather like the horror stories in the First World War about chopped-off children's hands and the eating of babies' corpses. But then the business stopped him sleeping, especially as he believed the Nazis capable of any base act, and so he started searching around. As a 'laid-off' civil servant, he had all the time in the world, as well as connections with people in the resistance. Nevertheless, nearly three months passed before he could be certain that the BBC report corresponded to reality. I said that I was recounting the episode because the person who eventually explained things to my father and even, if my memory serves me right, mentioned or produced some evidence (the Gerstein Report?) had been Herr L., 'a senior member of staff at the Speer ministry'.

Speer was not in the least surprised. Naturally, as he has since discovered, quite a few of his people knew at least from rumours what had been happening. In all government offices, he claimed without hesitation, those 'down below' are usually better informed than the people 'at the top', where the air is thinner and there is less knowledge of details. This has to be accepted as the general experience. But doubts remain about Speer's lack of knowledge.

===== Heidelberg. Speer said one often hears that Hitler was cold in his personal relations and entirely fixated on power. That is right but also wrong. He had a side where feelings were dominant, or anyway a strong element of sentimentality. Mussolini should be mentioned first of all. At some moment (around the end of 1944) he heard Hitler say that he had 'sacrificed victory to his friendship for the Duce', and perhaps that is not altogether wrong. But, to Speer's surprise, even Streicher was one of them, as were the gauleiters Sauckel, Kaufmann, Bürckel and all the so-called Old Fighters. He noticed this in autumn 1943 after his speech in Poznań,[3] in which he had once more challenged the gauleiters and read the riot act to them in a tone he had scarcely ever adopted before. The next day, Hitler received the gauleiters at a session of 'rhetorical massage treatment', as those close to him called it, and he later had a private talk with some of them. He then changed overnight towards him [Speer], becoming for no reason vehement and irritable. Soon afterwards he even shouted at him in an agitated way.

By the way, Speer added that he soon discovered the argument that the gauleiters had used to win over Hitler. On the one hand, they all untruthfully protested that he (Speer) had threatened them with a concentration camp. Some also took the view that he had walked into the trap 'of industry' and become its puppet. The Führer was 'too trusting', and after the turn in the war had always been receptive to that idea.

It was put forward especially by those gauleiters who, in the early years, had belonged to the socialist wing of the Party and still harboured 'anti-capitalist yearnings'. Another claim that impressed Hitler was that 'my repeated demands to shut down some consumer industry plants' had nothing to do with the war, but merely reflected the pressure of powerful corporations 'in whose pocket' he [Speer] was supposed to be.

One of the effects of the Poznań failure was that in future Hitler instructed Saur to ring through the production figures that he had previously asked Speer to provide over the telephone. Hitler never explained why he was doing this but simply got one of his secretaries to choose another number.

===== In his time as a minister, Speer states, he soon discovered how to get his various demands accepted. If Hitler denied some request, he stayed away from the Führer's headquarters for several days, until he heard through von Below, Brandt or whomever that Hitler was getting 'impatient' and had asked about him on several occasions. He would then make his appearance as unexpectedly as possible and, during a discussion that usually began in a self-consciously cool and practical spirit, would as if by chance pull out an architectural sketch lying seemingly overlooked among the armaments papers. Hitler's attention would be immediately aroused, but Speer would pretend that that was not the right time for it. Hitler became even more interested and wanted to know more details, so that they became increasingly caught up in one of their conversations about architecture and were unable to stop. In the end, the appointment lasted much longer than it had been scheduled for. Then he packed up his papers, not without calmly asking on his way out whether the decision that had recently gone against him could be reversed. In most cases Hitler then complied with his request.

The apparently simple trick even worked after the critical days in Poznań, in autumn 1943, when for a while during their discussions of the situation Hitler repeatedly gave him an angry look and seemed not to know how things should stand between them. Basically, any clear-headed person would have seen through his game. But, strangely enough, not Hitler. As soon as he had seen the drawing, the 'Show it to me!' came out as if at a push of a button – and minutes later the old collegiality between them had reappeared and a relieved Hitler lost himself in the plans and went into raptures. As a rule, he eventually became almost cordial. In fact, Speer had his greatest success in the tense days after Poznań. He brought with him not just one drawing but a whole bundle, in case the worst came to the worst and he was asked to tender his resignation. He spread the bunch of papers on the table in front of Hitler, and again he seemed immediately transformed. In the end, he took things to the limit, as it were, and secured Hitler's agreement – against the clear will of the gauleiters – that he would be given responsibility after the war for reconstruction of the destroyed cities. When he later described the conversation to his people, he remarked that the architectural sketches were his 'amulet'. They protected him from all dangers.

After a pertinent comment by Siedler, Speer said that the way in which he had behaved was not quite as coolly tactical as it now sounds. In such manoeuvres, the idea of regaining Hitler's confidence or sounding him out certainly played a role. Had Hitler proved unapproachable, it would surely have meant a crisis between them – and, in autumn 1943, even an open break. In any event, partly out of disappointment, partly out of a sense of hurt, he had toyed at the time with the idea of abandoning ministerial office and politics altogether. At first this had not been a serious idea, only a passing mood, and he had felt alarmed by himself. He had, as it were, held up before him the inadmissibility of this impulse and concluded that he must not 'run away from the flag'.

The thought of giving everything up had come to him again in November 1943, when his ministry was hit by a bomb. That night, when he arrived with some colleagues at Pariser Platz and caught sight of the badly damaged buildings, he wondered what significance he should see in it: whether the hit pointed to the end of his period as a minister or general inspector of buildings. The only correct thought – that it indicated the approaching end of the war – did not occur to him at the time.

===== Today, when we came back to this theme, Speer asserted that the greatest spur for him to give up the ministry, and to leave politics altogether, had probably come after he visited the 'Dora' V-weapons factory in early December 1943. Then, too, they had only been impulses, especially strong when the growing burden of his duties had weighed all too heavily on him. But after the three incidents in rapid succession – the crisis following Poznań, the partial destruction of his ministry, and the visit to the Mittelwerk–Dora complex – he caught himself thinking more and more often of calling it a day. Unfortunately it remained a question of moods, and he has to reproach himself for not getting to the root of the matter.

Then something else came along. In view of the destruction of German cities, he began to be considerably attracted by the prospect of reconstruction work. Huge tasks lay in wait, in comparison with which all his current activity seemed pointless or even absurd. The architectural profession, which 'happened to be mine', was geared to constructive purposes. What he was then doing had nothing to do with that, and indeed ran strictly counter to it. Such thoughts had often preoccupied him when he spent the Christmas and New Year's Eve of 1943 in Lapland. The trip was nothing other than an escape, but 'unconscious, like everything at the time'. Perhaps he had needed a friend to help him make the leap. But who really had friends in those years?

Speer added that the lack of a wise and disinterested adviser may also have had to do with the fact that, by the time he returned from Lapland, he had almost overcome the moody thoughts of resignation and again settled down to his duties. Also, despite all the fluctuations in their relationship, he was too strongly attached to Hitler emotionally: 'The dreams were still alive', he concluded.

====== Speer further remarked that the so-called sketch trick proved its worth when Hitler, in the midst of their discussions, launched into one of his endless political tirades and – for example, on the occasion of a visit by Ante Pavelić, Ciano or Marshal Antonescu – began to speak of the strategic significance and reliability of certain allies, the fighting strength of the units under their command, the quality of the troop commanders, and countless other details. Now and

Hitler and Speer during a discussion of building plans

then Speer would turn to the files and read through them – nervously, restlessly, with a sense of desperation at the time passing aimlessly by. Hitler noticed this, but did not halt his flow of words. Once, around the summer of 1943, he had the idea of preparing an architectural sketch during one of Hitler's explanations, and he was immediately successful. From one moment to the next Hitler forgot all the Antonescus in the world and interested himself in the development of the drawing.

Speer added that he had to admit to feeling embarrassed about this impertinence. At the time he thought it basically impermissible and once mentioned it to his 'semi-friend' Dr Brandt. But Brandt replied by saying that such things were admissible, in order to free 'the Führer from a noticeable depression'. There was no other justification for it.

═════ Speer advised me to refer to Hitler's so-called cultural speeches in my work. At the time, they had not only made a deep impression on him at the level of rhetoric. Rather, they had revealed a lot about Hitler's character. (*Addendum fourteen days later*: meanwhile read some of these speeches, mostly given by Hitler at Party congresses. Bewildered by Speer's advice.)

═════ Again about Linz and Hitler's idea of being buried in the bell-tower overlooking the town. Impression that it still hurts Speer to think that Giesler got the contract for Linz. I said how mad Hitler's plan had been, but also how much in character: elevation even in death, as if he had wanted to enter eternity high above the world.

═════ Heidelberg, August 1967. Long discussion of youth and parental home. Feelings of reverence for his father, a certain reserve towards his overbearing mother. But he did not suffer because of home – he just felt strange there. Overall a happy youth. But then he grabbed the first opportunity to leave the world of Heidelberg and did not often return there, especially as relations became strained after he told his parents that he planned to marry Margarete Weber. In those days, Speer said, he was more like a child of nature, and when he went to university an academic child of nature; a youth movement type, a little hare-brained if you want to put it in a nutshell. He thought that many others were like that; he was not an exception. 'Nature' was something like the 'fashionable happiness' of the time, whereas civilization was the 'fashionable hate' of those years.

Politics was a taboo subject at home: it was simply not done to speak about it, any more than about what people did in bed or about money matters. Strictly speaking, politics was mentioned only in connection with the unpleasantness that the relatives from Mainz had to endure from the French authorities.[4] He had naturally heard about the Kaiser's abdication, the Revolution and the Treaty of Versailles. But all that had happened far away and scarcely impinged on Heidelberg and its Schloss Wolfsbrunnenweg.

Conversations repeatedly turned to the subject of Versailles, but less at home than with schoolfriends, teachers or the Webers and later at university. There was a lot of scorn and contempt for the 'West'. He never forgot the phrase 'clown's cap' (with which the republic was said to have returned from Versailles) and felt a corresponding sense of 'humiliation', although for a long time he did not know at all what a humiliation, indeed a 'national' humiliation, actually meant.

People have no idea 'how deep that ran', Speer said. Later he sometimes thought that a kind of 'national community' [*Volksgemeinschaft*] had taken shape in those days, which Hitler had only to organize. His bitterness against the left stemmed not least from the fact that many of its spokesmen had trivialized the humiliation of the Versailles treaty. 'I too felt indignant about it.' But studies, concerts and rambling trips were more important to him in the end. And then the unsettling feeling that there was no solid ground anywhere in the world. That got a grip on everyone. One thing in particular that he learned in those years of youth, when you were supposed to acquire 'a secure footing', was a capacity 'to live with contradictions and not feel their incompatibility'.

All that is more or less in the manuscript, Speer said. What he has not written down, for understandable reasons, is that during the period of the Great Depression and mass unemployment that followed his studies he saw himself as 'a child favoured by destiny'. He never had any doubt that he would make his way in life and achieve 'something great, something spectacular'. Of course, that is the case with nearly all ambitious young men. But unlike his fellow students, for example, he was always fairly sure of getting there, however much his vain efforts over some contract or other temporarily made him despair.

▬▬▬ 'My "apolitical" attitude is not, as it is repeatedly claimed, a retrospective invention of mine or my defence counsel at Nuremberg, Dr Fläschner', Speer remarked. Hitler too for a long time (perhaps always) saw in him the non-political expert. Anyway, during the years when he belonged to Hitler's innermost circle, he was not once called in to offer political advice about a specific issue, such as the annexation of Austria and even less the occupation of Prague and everything that followed. Not that he wanted to have a say. But sometimes he wondered whether Hitler took him seriously in any matter other than architecture. He certainly did not have any 'mysterious solemnity' and reflected on why Ribbentrop, for example, did have it.

I said that, even with an 'apolitical' attitude, one can still exert a disastrous political influence. Speer retorted that that applied only to the realm of facts. He, however, had built a moral accusation out of his attitude. No agreement.

▬▬▬ A couple of additional remarks on the days in Obersalzberg, which Speer, as I said to him, described very vividly in the manuscript. He took the little compliment as a knightly accolade.

The idler's instinct had had no place at all in his life, Speer added. It had been filled with conferences, professional duties, discussions of building projects and a thousand and one appointments. The complete split between hectic official duties and passive conduct of life often made him extremely jittery and took a toll on his health. To make the excruciating days (and especially evenings) a little more stimulating, he suggested that interesting scientists or artists should be invited to the 'mountain' – for example, an architect in his employ, Arno Breker, a Wagner connoisseur, a museum expert such as Hans Posse, director of the Dresden Art Gallery, the deep-sea diver Hans Hass (who was talked about a lot at the time), and so on. But Hitler had already rejected such proposals in Berlin, and when Speer once returned to them a few days later Hitler 'almost agitatedly told him to stop'.

For a long time he had been unable to explain this, especially as Hitler had broad interests ranging from art and architecture through music and cultural history to all manner of cosmic theories. Only after some time did he realize that Hitler needed the emptiness of those days to counterbalance the pressure of his semi-public existence. Speer agreed that it probably also worried Hitler that, as chancellor, he would have to say farewell to the old bohemian habits. Another factor, presumably, was that he had to collect himself for each of his successive adventures. Speer said: 'In those days he was playing a game of chance, and he knew it.'

By the way, Speer added, Hitler's martial fancies were repeatedly inflamed by the Untersberg opposite the Berghof, where legend had it that Emperor Barbarossa lay asleep. 'It's no accident', Hitler liked to say. He saw a 'vocation' in the fact that his private residence lay opposite 'the emperor's mountain'. Quite often late in the day, after he had taken leave of the idle round, he went over to the large window and stared for a couple of minutes at the dark shape of the mountain.

═══ On being asked, Speer thought that especially at the beginning he had often felt in a completely alien world in Obersalzberg. Hitler and the people around him spoke about issues and contexts that lay far outside his own field of vision.

Their way of speaking about politics, about fundamentals, about a particular situation or a hypothetical scenario was as unfamiliar to him as Hitler's judgement about people. A great coldness and detachment. But at the time he thought that that was how a politician had to look at things.

Speer added that the central consideration was always tactical expediency and, with regard to individuals, their usefulness for certain tasks. Until then, Speer added, things which 'had nothing to do with my interests had soon tired or bored me'. But there it was different. They fascinated him, and the very fact that many ways of seeing things made him feel a little uneasy actually strengthened their allure. In the end, Hitler was nothing less than the centre of international politics – or, as they sometimes put it, the 'mover of the world'. That gave them too a certain importance, as they recognized not without pride.

===== Later. For all that, Speer said, it should be borne in mind that he was again and again enthralled by Hitler's obsession with architecture, and that this overcame any doubts that sometimes welled up inside him. It was almost with a kind of mania that Hitler proposed sketches for new city planning or large building projects, for fortresses and bunkers, 'again and again bunkers', and the staff were constantly 'on the go' fetching various papers, designs, city views or drawings.

This often went on for days, even through the night. Once, it must have been around 1936, Hitler asked whether in anticipation – that is, before the new plan for the whole of Berlin – a new Reich Chancellery should not be built that did justice to the regained power of the Reich. But such ideas came and went, driven mainly by the grand projects that were his great passion. However much he shared the intoxication of planning, he sometimes felt that the hours of discussion were holding him up (since they often went around in circles), and even that they were a torture. 'But I say that today', he added, as if lost in thought.

===== Speer mentioned Hitler's liking for failed heroes: Rienzi,[5] Holländer,[6] Siegfried. Also for Hanns Johst's betrayed 'king',[7] which he saw on the stage around that time: 'It became clear to me that, above all else, he recognized himself in these figures and perhaps even foresaw his own end in them.'

===== Speer is convinced that Hitler had a 'bedroom affair' with Winifred Wagner[8] – as he put it with slight embarrassment. On the way between Munich and Berlin (or vice versa) they often stopped over in Bad Berneck. Hitler then immediately set off for Bayreuth and returned late at night, usually around five or six in the morning. Speer cannot believe that he spoke with Winifred only about the festival, its financial difficulties (which he generously solved), directors, conductors or the master himself. His suspicions were aroused by, among other things, the fact that Hitler and Winifred called each other *du* in private and switched to *Sie* as soon as another person was present. In this alternation, they always gave the impression of being caught in the act; one almost thought that one saw them blushing. Speer thinks that Hitler never got beyond his puberty stage and that this secretiveness was for him part of all erotic activity. Perhaps he could not imagine a serious relationship between a man and a woman without feelings of prohibition. I added that this may have been the attraction of the relationship with his niece Geli Raubal, since the ban on incest is certainly one of the most imaginatively arousing.

In the course of the discussion, Speer reported that there had even been talk of one or more offers of marriage, which Hitler made to his 'queen', as he liked to call Winifred. They were before his appointment as chancellor, shortly after Geli Raubal's suicide, but Winifred is said to have rejected his proposals. Speer, however, could not and would not vouch for all this. I mentioned that I had recently met Friedelind Wagner, who answered my question on the subject in the purest Frankish dialect: 'Hitler was on for it alright, but not Winifred.'

Nevertheless, Speer looked somewhat confused when I eventually laughed at these conjectures and spoke of 'non-sense' and 'casino gossip'. He thought that at the time, after his return, Hitler had given the impression of being (he searched for the right word) 'satisfied'. I objected that this may have had to do with Bayreuth as such, with the recognition he found there, the scope for sponsorship that it gave him, and other things besides. After all, they had been friends since 1923, and through Winfried Hitler had received assistance, encouragement and social status. One also heard it said, Speer interjected, that she gave Hitler the decisive stimulus to take *Mein Kampf* beyond a draft about which his intentions had initially been unclear. As far as the 'love story' was concerned, I pointed out that from the mid-1930s there had also been Heinz Tietjen, whom Hitler might, but Winifred certainly would not, have disregarded.

But Speer did not give up his view. 'In those days at least', he said in conclusion, 'I was quite sure of it, because of count-less little revealing signs.' The next morning, Hitler always appeared unusually buoyant, with a sparkle in his eyes – joyful even. Speer waved aside the repeated objection that it was not necessarily a 'bedroom affair', that the Wahnfried Villa might have been a kind of cultural 'tabernacle' for Hitler. If Hitler was now and then jittery or ill-tempered for days on end, his entourage jokingly remarked that the Führer really did need another 'Bayreuth course of treatment'. Well then!

===== About Hitler's relationship with Eva Braun, why he admitted her to the court at all, and other matters relating to Obersalzberg. Speer thought that the mystery of their relationship was easy to unravel, if there was anything like a mystery at all. Hitler 'kept' his 'Fräulein Braun' (as he always called her) exclusively for certain natural needs that even he could not ignore – for the 'regulation of his hormone balance', as it were.

The teacher's daughter from Munich, whom Hitler met through Heinrich Hoffmann,[9] was simple and unassuming – and 'full of the joys of life', as the expression goes – but she also had an uncomplaining character, so that Hitler could scarcely have found anyone more suited to the role he had in mind. Undoubtedly she loved the 'Führer' (as she called him in the presence of others) with complete devotion, whereas Speer was convinced that Hitler mustered no real feelings for her, except perhaps during the last days in the bunker. But then they were mainly feelings of gratitude for her devotion and her willingness to accompany him into death. And a few more things like that. When I asked Speer how he knew all this, he replied that he obviously could not produce any proof, but that when you are constantly with someone for twelve years or so you do not need proof; you just know things.

When I laughed, Speer looked half surprised and half irritated. I told him that, a while before, I had had a telephone conversation on the same subject with Hitler's former foreign press boss, Ernst 'Putzi' Hanfstaengl, who gave me a totally different account of Hitler's sex life. In his view, Hitler was such an egomaniac that he was incapable of mustering even the 'little loving care' for another person that the sexual act requires. Manically obsessed as he was with the Will, he was able to shut out, and did shut out, even involuntary, instinctive reactions. In short, Hitler was 'a born onanist'. It was 'quite certain' that he had never had the slightest sexual contact with Eva Braun. That was 'unthinkable', Hanfstaengl shouted. 'Never, ever!' 'Eva' was just a 'status darling'. You had to keep something like her in that chummy male company, especially during the years when the movement was on the rise and struggling. Precisely because he was the 'Führer', Hitler could not do otherwise. Eva Braun was just part of the scenery; everyone talked about how she spent the nights alone during Hitler's visits to Obersalzberg, and so on.

And now, I said to Speer, you must hear the reasons for my amusement. When Hanfstaengl was asked how he knew all these things, he answered: 'Well, look, you don't need to have a bright lamp to shine on them. When you've been together on a daily basis with someone for twelve years or more, including the time in jail at Landsberg and a lot of trips, you just know them.'

This little episode also tells us a lot about the value and credibility of contemporaries or 'eye witnesses'.

======= Hitler's love for music. Only Wagner, march music and operetta, Speer thought. Sometimes he used to wonder what music meant to Hitler: whether it was not in fact a means of conveyance for great scenes. Anyway, he dismissed all chamber music with a contemptuous wave of the hand. Once he surprised Speer by telling him that he had drawn colour sketches for all the scenes in *The Ring*. He got someone to fetch them, but then, with sudden disgruntlement, broke off the inspection and almost hurriedly collected the drawings together – probably because Speer had referred to the important stage designer Alfred Roller, whose work in Vienna and Bayreuth was an unmistakable model in Hitler's towering sets. When Speer asked to be shown the drawings again, Hitler always used some pretext to put him off; he had evidently been piqued by his indeed somewhat 'tactless remark', as he did not wish to have any models. Early in 1939, he did tell him that he was sketching some stage sets for *Lohengrin*, but Speer never saw them. Perhaps Hitler had been unhappy with what he came up with. Or else he had not wanted to risk a second critical judgement.

The most powerful effect on Hitler was produced by the conclusion of *Götterdämmerung*. Whenever the 'raging flames' soared up to the dying figure of Brünnhilde, he leant across to Frau Winifred in their box and kissed her hand with visible emotion.

━━━ Speer reported that, when once, despite Hitler's well-known aversion, he had suggested inviting Richard Strauss to the Berghof, Hitler grew increasingly irritable and finally said that he had tried on various occasions to have the composer's works banned, since 'he' went along with all the 'newfangled screeching'. Speer suspected that the main reason why Hitler had stopped short of a ban was not the reputation that Strauss enjoyed in wide circles. Rather, as many of his remarks indicated, he had cast his mind back to the early years in Vienna, when even influential members of the bourgeoisie had greatly appreciated Richard Strauss as a musician and considered him the legitimate heir of Richard Wagner. Whenever a table guest mentioned his name, however, Hitler let it be known that Strauss had no feel for the great stage scene that was Wagner's legacy.

Speer remembered something else that Hitler once said: 'Strauss is of no interest to me as a composer. Completely second-rate!' This also meant that the ruler's respectful courting went out only to the man whose name was honoured all over the world. It was also often mentioned at tea that Strauss was an opponent of the regime. 'We had to boot him out soon enough as president of the Reich Music Chamber', Hitler said in his crude way. Strauss had got much too involved with the 'Jewish riff-raff'.[10]

Speer himself had sometimes thought in connection with Richard Strauss that Hitler was engaging in rather too many 'big fat lies'. But – by way of excusing at least himself – he readily made the point that a politician is forced into a thousand untruths and that perhaps constant lying on all sides eventually affects the light in which he is seen. It should also be considered that when Hitler thought of someone he always had in mind how he might be politically useful. At the same time – continued Speer, in his to-and-fro train of thought – each of Hitler's remarks about Strauss contained the most scornful judgement of the celebrated composer of *Salome*, *Der Rosenkavalier* and the great tone poems.

But – Speer concluded after being asked – he had expressed none of the things that went through his head about Hitler's disparaging remarks on Richard Strauss. It would have angered Hitler too much, since he thought of himself as the highest authority on musical questions. 'I didn't risk it!' he said. More than he ever suspected, another consideration was probably the danger to the unique opportunities that Hitler offered him. Who can say for sure that they would have been prepared to risk it, he added shortly after, 'except, of course, for the people I meet at every step nowadays'?

===== During the conversations in Obersalzberg, Hitler often displayed a tendency to make disparaging remarks about people not present or to imitate their gestures and modes of expression. He even spoke scornfully about loyal comrades from the old days of whom he had been fond. If they found themselves in real difficulties, however, he stood by them and even covered up cases of graft or corruption.

The reason for Hitler's disparagement of others was never completely clear to Speer. Perhaps it was misanthropy, or perhaps his superiority complex. No one was supposed to measure up to him. Not the least argument in favour of this is the fact that successful Party people were often his favourite objects of scorn.

He finds it hard to forgive himself that he often laughed along with these 'stupid jokes', especially when Hitler mimicked old comrades-in-arms with a certain 'cabaret skill'. In those days politeness dictated some display of amusement. But sometimes it occurred to him afterwards that he had betrayed his dignity when Hitler imitated the toadying zeal of Heinrich Hoffmann or the lecturing Teutonic speech of Himmler and everyone burst into laughter. The tastelessness struck him most forcefully when Hitler crudely derided poor Unity Mitford (who tried to follow him everywhere) as 'Unity Mitfahrt':[11] 'That was more or less the level!'

Speer added that this is why his behaviour now seems to him unforgivable, and sometimes he thinks that he already reproached himself for it at the time. But he is not at all sure. For it is really very difficult to put yourself in a state of mind that you felt in the past. 'Often you make yourself baser than you were. More often better. It's nearly always wrong.'

▬▬ It was the cinema which suggested to Speer the idea of the Lichtdom, the cathedral of light that he regards as his most significant inspiration. It was not his own invention, but he was the first to recognize the political usefulness of the play of light, its power to command rapt attention. In the end, all he did was imitate the spectacle that the navy sometimes performed at the end of manoeuvres. But film was more important. During one trip to the cinema, it occurred to him that technical means could be used to produce uplifting moods that would appear not 'Wagnerish' but modern and in keeping with the times. All he had to do then was implement this, and he found it especially easy because the link between technology and emotion corresponded to what he himself felt.

———— Sylt. October 1967. It struck me that 30 January 1933 scarcely featured in the manuscript, and I asked Speer why. He replied that he barely noticed the day in Heidelberg or Mannheim, where he was staying at the time – or anyway did not see it as the victory of Hitler and the Party (to which he had belonged since March 1931). It was just a change of chancellor, similar to many others before. On the matter that many had experienced it as a decisive turning point, he said that perhaps they had been mistaken. It was also possible, however, that he had suppressed or anyway downplayed his reaction. After all, nearly forty years had passed since then. Like most people, his only wish had been for things to get better in Germany, and by God things had certainly not been good. 'That was really all.' And he trusted Hitler more than any other politician to do it. In this sense he had expectations. But certainly doubts too, though to a lesser extent. At least that is what he thinks. And, incidentally, the Mannheim Party organization had been a 'dreadful crowd of petty bourgeois'. 'Petty gestures, big words.'

———— Some more about the strange company in Obersalzberg, which disparaged everyone involved. Finally Speer said that as alien to him as most of 'those people' had been the ideological convictions they revealed, at least in conversation. He did not know whether they actually believed in them. 'For everyone, only Hitler was beyond all debate.' Every single one of them was unconditionally devoted to him.

Speer's devotion was further strengthened by the visible evidence that even Hitler did not take seriously the talk about age-old Germanic culture, runes, *Thingtheater*,[12] and so on. Once, in Hitler's presence during tea at the Berghof,

Hitler and Speer in a moment of evident disharmony in Obersalzberg, summer 1939

he had let slip the remark that all that was 'humbug', and for a moment, as silence suddenly descended on the whole party, he was horrified by his own presumption. Hitler didn't quite catch the remark and, turning to Hewel (or Brandt?) seated next to him, asked: 'What did Speer say?' With a bright-red face, the man repeated the phrase as if he himself had been caught in the act. Hitler seemed to reflect for a brief moment. Then he gave a laugh and said reassuringly: 'Don't worry, Speer! I think the same about it.' And, as if to a cue, the whole party that had just been sitting there stunned let out a sigh of relief and cast appreciative glances at him.

===== In relation to the company at Obersalzberg, Speer let slip one remark that he immediately tried to tone down. He said that he had 'never had problems' with arrogance. This may well be the most astonishing change of all that has come over him. Today he behaves modestly, unpretentiously, one might almost say humbly. Role-playing? Unlikely, although one often hears this said.

===== Speer brought along some photos that are supposed to go into the book. The most surprising one is of Hitler and Speer sitting on a bench in Obersalzberg, visibly disgruntled with each other. 'A picture of estranged lovers', I commented, not without irony. Speer was taken aback and looked at me with a frown of annoyance. I added by way of explanation that no one would think the photo showed a leader with his devoted follower. The two people in it are not that, or not mainly that. The photo reveals an intimacy unthinkable between Hitler and any of his other henchmen. 'It's a sulky couple', I added. 'Would Hitler ever have sulked with Goering or Himmler? He'd simply have chased them away. In any case, nothing else I know shows so plainly the exceptional position, based not least on erotic elements, which you had in the Hitler entourage.'

Speer, who to begin with had suspected me of wanting to imply an actively homoerotic or even covertly homosexual relationship between him and Hitler, lost his initial sense of annoyance, especially when Siedler said some words to calm him down. We started talking about his personal relations with Hitler. He conceded that on Hitler's side an emotional, perhaps even erotic factor had played some role, although he had obvious problems with the word 'erotic'. In the end, he admitted that he too had not been guided 'only by practical motives' such as admiration for the great man, architectural projects and so on. Once he even used the word 'friendship' to describe their relationship, and pointed out how often since then it had been thrown back at him.

Incidentally, Speer could no longer remember what had led to the quarrel on the bench. If his memory did not deceive him, they had argued because of Bormann, who at that time, precisely through the ruining of Obersalzberg, was beginning to put himself forward not least as the 'man for everything'. Hitler regularly defended Bormann, and differences appeared between him and Speer on several occasions because of the all-powerful secretary. 'There were not really any other causes, leaving aside the period around the end of 1943.'

Speer further reported something Hettlage had said after watching him in conversation with Hitler, as they went across with some sketches to the recently built Model Street. After Hitler had left, Hettlage said: 'Herr Speer, you must know you are Hitler's unhappy love.' Speer said that he was completely taken aback and asked Hettlage what he meant. Hettlage shrugged and simply replied: 'You should think that it has a good and a bad side!' When Speer wanted an explanation for that too, he merely shook his head and uttered not another word. Speer added that at the time he had often puzzled over what Hettlage had really meant, and that he had not been able to get his remarks out of his head. 'Today I know what he meant.'

═══ Speer said that, in their architectural discussions in Obersalzberg, Hitler liked to point to the nearby Salzburg fortress, which had never been captured. It was his view that every building they set to work on should arouse this feeling in the beholder: it should appear great, powerful and impregnable, and convey feelings of protection as strong as the idea that any rebellion was pointless.

═══ On the question of whether Hitler had ever displayed in their conversations any knowledge of architecture or architectural history, Speer said: 'In general, no more than an appropriately educated layman.' Hitler had known more about the nineteenth century, although nearly all of it came from reading and only a little from opinions he had formed himself. Of course he had been familiar with Semper, his heroes Helmer and Fellner, Garnier and many others, including a number of second-rate architects. Also Hofmann, Loos, Wagner and the so-called Vienna School, whose work he described as 'architectural crime' or 'factory art'. Hitler had a similar view of Mussolini's architects and master builders, of Nervi, Piacentini, Terragni and any others he knew.

Sometimes, Speer said, he had the impression that Hitler prepared himself for their discussions by reading various things, or raised questions in connection with what he had just been reading. Once he directly broached the issue of whether there was a general language of architecture beyond all particular styles, and what advantages and disadvantages resulted from the academic compulsion to impose form. Then again he got worked up about the arbitrariness of modern artists, which led them to produce really 'nasty things' in painting and architecture; he regularly mentioned the Bauhaus and said that fortunately people would never learn to live with its 'glass coops'. In a calmer mood, he might ask whether the new architecture was in principle suited to technically functional buildings; at least that could be discussed, but it was completely wrong for state buildings and emblematic structures. Hitler soon grew tired of such wide-ranging discussions, however, as he was all too fixed in his views and completely in the grip of a few prejudices.

⸻ Next day. Speer made some additional points about the architectural discussions with Hitler, for which he had jotted down a few notes. Hitler repeatedly stated that, in relation to every building, his aim was to make the spirit of contemporary reality vividly present to future generations.

Nothing recalled the great ages of history more vigorously than their buildings. What would the world know of the Roman Empire and the emperors without the architecture they left behind? After periods of decline, 'the feeling for national greatness' could be revived 'only through monumental buildings'.

===== In their discussions, Speer added today, Hitler showed his ability to grasp a sketch quickly and to connect up the ground plan with individual aspects into a vivid picture. Even if months had passed, he immediately found his bearings when a new submission was made for one of the fifteen or more projects that were always on the go, and he could recall the agreed changes as they affected town or regional planning and even the details of particular façades.

Although Hitler usually adopted an imperious tone towards his political collaborators, he was almost collegial during their architectural discussions and expressed his wish for changes in a more friendly or sometimes even inquiring manner. If one of the gauleiters, district leaders or mayors around him tried to have a say, or actually spoke out, he not infrequently cut him off in a visibly hurtful way. Even Bormann – who was then, of course, not as powerful as during the war – came in for the treatment on a few occasions when he did no more than agree with Hitler's opinion, being so firmly 'cut short' that he soon left the room on some pretext or other.

===== Speer can still hear Hitler's frequent explanations – as if to justify the length of an architectural discussion they had just had – that he needed this activity not only for relaxation but even more to gain the strength for his political undertakings. He used his own discretion in awarding contracts to the ten or so architects who belonged to the inner circle. 'My privileged position', Speer said, 'was expressed in the fact that he often invited me to attend meetings with other architects.'

Hitler tirelessly drew sketches during their discussions. Though quickly dashed off, they did not lack skill and were perspectively accurate; he was able to draw ground plans, sketches and elevations perfectly true to scale. Sometimes, the morning after a discussion, he would produce a detailed sketch that he had prepared overnight.

Most of the drawings, however, originated in a few hurried strokes during a discussion. As Hitler left the work lying around at the end, Speer or another of those present usually took charge of it. Speer still has the sheets that came into his possession in this way: he has numbered all 125 pieces in the collection and supplied each of them with a subject description. It is remarkable, he concluded, that more than a quarter relate to the building projects in Linz, which were obviously especially close to Hitler's heart. There are also numerous theatre designs.

===== To the question whether the comparatively moderate proportions of the new Reich Chancellery, visibly more severe than the buildings on the Grosse Strasse/Berlin, were not ultimately inspired by Troost and constituted a late tribute to Hitler's favourite architect, Speer replied: 'No, anyway not consciously.' As an architect one did not think of that sort of thing. There were too many inherent laws that had to be observed. In that case, time pressure and the 'pretty awkward shape' of the plot of land available on Voss-Strasse had played a major role – anyway, certainly greater than any thought of Troost. And, perhaps detecting in my words some praise for the new Reich Chancellery, he reciprocated that it had been fairly successful. But even today he considers that, as far as the buildings are concerned, the Nürnberger Anlage was better. 'My most important work.'

Nevertheless, he had been proud and happy when, during their first round of inspection, he noticed the admiring glances that Hitler repeatedly cast at him. He observed the same sparkle in Hitler's eyes years later, when he assumed responsibility for the armaments ministry and took the first rigorous measures. 'Don't let anyone take the fight out of you', Hitler had said to him encouragingly; and he had looked almost grateful in response to his energetic agreement.

───── 'The buildings we planned for Berlin, as well as Nuremberg, were all places of worship', Speer remarked. 'Devotional architecture.' Sometimes he saw Hitler's proposals (which always underlay this character of the work) as an expression of his Catholicism, completely secularized, of course. But he has kept his appreciation for spaces that create a sense of sublimeness or solemnity.

3

HIGHS AND LOWS

December 1967, Heidelberg. Difference of opinion with Speer about the self-characterizations scattered through the manuscript. They are too general and explain nothing, I said critically. I also mentioned that I would like to know how, in winter 1943 or at the latest spring 1944, after a long period of completely heteronomous existence, he arrived at such a surprisingly independent, even rebellious attitude towards Hitler; and how it came about that, both at Nuremberg and in Spandau, he developed and stubbornly maintained such a personal profile in comparison with his fellow prisoners. For me that was something like the puzzle of his life, and as he wanted to publish an autobiography rather than an account of his times he would have to explain this break.

Speer was evidently surprised by the emphasis I laid on these points, although I tried to strike a certain affability in my tone. He scarcely knew what to reply, then said that he would like to think it over. In the end he asked whether my view did not place a question mark over the whole concept of the book, as it had been taking shape until then.

===== Later in the hotel room, alone with Siedler. He defended Speer and said it was anyway remarkable that he had never offered the standard justification of nearly all the other perpetrators: that he had been a mere cog in a huge machine.

I objected that such an argument might conflict with Speer's sense of pride, and that perhaps he had never even attained that kind of distance from himself. Many of the things he said implied that, even today, he feels it as a kind of stroke of luck to have been part of a vast machinery as well as something like one of the forces driving it. To many people the pleasure of functioning smoothly means more than any degree of autonomous decision. Speer is evidently one such person and does not wish to belittle himself with any talk of being a 'cog'.

===== Schloss Korb, March 1968. Returned with Siedler from a trip to Italy together. We asked Speer about Paestum, where we had just been and where he went thirty years ago. He went into raptures for a moment. 'Paestum made the strongest impression in those days, perhaps the most perfect architectural complex I had ever seen. Unforgettable still today, and even more overwhelming than Castel del Monte, which also made a deep impression on me. Paestum left me stunned and speechless, simply standing there in its natural grandeur. Of what building can you say that?' He has always regretted that they did not experience the much-praised evening when the sun appears to fall between the temples into the sea.

Of course, he added, he had been aware how remote his own designs were from 'the spirit of those structures'. But from then on he had had a 'living' model for the goals he had previously pursued only 'in a kind of darkness', basing himself 'on photographs and descriptions': 'the Doric world', he said, in an almost solemn tone. For him it has always stood high above all the much-admired palaces of the Renaissance. And, when he or his colleagues deviated from it (as they did with the 'flourishes' on the Grosse Strasse), it has weighed on his conscience ever since.

━━━━━ After his father's visit to Berlin, when he showed him the Model Street, he often asked why his rejection of it had been so unusually violent. 'You've gone completely crazy!' his father had said, with both him and Hitler in mind. Once Speer even tried to get him to explain. 'But my father would not be drawn into anything and simply looked at me quizzically, as if to say that any discussion was pointless if I couldn't see it myself.'

━━━━━ Today Speer said that he sometimes joked with close colleagues like Wolters about Hitler's 'record-breaking' madness. To the question of why he went along with it, and even surpassed it in various ways, he answered with an almost helpless laughter.

He actually reinforced the question by remarking that Hitler had seemed 'almost scared' on being presented with the sketch for the Grosse Halle and had raised objections about the load-bearing capacity of the cupola. But when he, Speer, pointed out that the static issues had been examined and satisfactorily resolved, Hitler 'gave his enthusiastic agreement'.

━━━━━ From 1937 on, after their architectural discussions (especially those concerning the model section), one repeatedly heard Hitler say in a kind of sigh: 'If only I were healthy!' He expressed the same concerns on the night of his fiftieth birthday, standing before the model of the triumphal arch. 'All of us who belonged to his inner circle suspected that he had received disturbing indications from his doctors; perhaps there had also been some hints from Morell, who before long joined the "Berghof Group".'

In any event, he once more seemed to be filled with forebodings of death. Now and then, however, it had occurred to Speer that Hitler was using such bouts of hypochondria to justify his restlessness, to urge on his entourage (including military people) and to push them into greater haste.

====== Speer said that in spring 1939, when he and his wife returned from their trip to Italy, his mother (who had been looking after their children) told him that she been invited almost every day to the Berghof. Hitler had been extremely attentive to her and turned on the Viennese charm, though in an almost embarrassingly conventional manner – like someone who, though not himself kind, would like to give the impression that he is. Anyway, sometimes he almost made her forget that she was seated next to 'the great Leader'. Leaving aside the artificiality of his manner, Hitler behaved in a way that was modest rather than grandiose. She was surprised to find that everything he said was rather inconsequential.

She further said that the house furnishings, the parties for guests and the whole ceremony during and after meals struck her as dreadfully petty bourgeois, or, to be more precise, as falsely bourgeois in a strange, petty-bourgeois way. Everything left a convoluted impression, as it were. 'I wouldn't have liked to see in my own home any of those who were gathered together there', she said. Of course, some people who came to visit them also spoke too loudly, bowed too deeply or tried to draw the staff into conversation. 'But sometimes we couldn't get out of inviting people like that. He, on the other hand . . .?' Despite this experience, however, she had kept her

admiration for Hitler. Great people should be measured with
different yardsticks. 'Who knows', she added, 'what things
were like at Bismarck's or Napoleon's social evenings!'

I suggested to Speer that he should include this account in
his *Memoirs*. But, quite uncharacteristically, he rejected this
with an almost violent determination. He refused to tell me
the reasons.

====== When he stood for the first time before St Peter's in
Rome, Speer was amazed and disappointed at the same time.
'It was almost like a nightmare experience.' The structure
and the square in front of it, with Bernini's famous colon-
nade, struck him as almost 'intimate' against the background
of the plans for Berlin and Nuremberg: 'How small it
seemed to me!' Photos and film shots had given him a sense
of how far from the crowd the pope stood when, for example, he pronounced his *urbi et orbi* blessing. Hitler would
have to bridge an even greater distance. 'For a moment I
asked myself whether we had gone too far.'

He then had calculations made about the extent to which
photography increased the real distances. Leni Riefenstahl,
to whom he occasionally turned for advice, held the view
that photos doubled the impression of distance in comparison with reality. 'This reassured me. A chance experience
should not undo the plans I had made, which in the end were
Hitler's plans too.'

====== Hitler was the typical autodidact, Speer said today.
This was already apparent in his style of argument: he always
began by showering, or intimidating, the other person with
a plethora of supposedly irrefutable facts and statistical
columns. 'But he did not grasp anything by working on it, or
pay any heed to contrary arguments. He would then combine
whatever served his purpose with bold, often truly impressive

theses. They were really overwhelming, enough to break down all defences. Then there was the suggestive manner in which he expressed himself. Impossible to forget or describe the curiously breathless way in which he stated his beliefs, even when it was a matter of quite secondary issues.'

===== Hitler's fondness for metaphors from the ancient world also revealed him as an autodidact. He called Pericles his model, equated himself with Alexander as a conqueror, with Caesar as a founder of cities, and so on down to Friedrich Barbarossa and Cosimo, the *pater patriae*. If he opposed the creation of a reserve position, as he did after Stalingrad, he referred to the burnt ships of the Greeks. And, towards the end of the war, he repeatedly drew on the same example – not least in the constant disputes over the construction of a fighter force and its deployment against Allied 'terror attacks' in summer 1944. Every destroyed city is like a burnt ship, he once said; on closer examination, destruction actually helps us, and besides we shall build the cities to be more beautiful than they were. When the ring closed around Berlin in March–April 1945 he liked to refer to Leonidas and the Spartans (who also fought and held out in a desperate situation) or sometimes to the Ostrogoths at Vesuvius.[1] Speer said that he called it 'autosuggestion through myths'. And, along with all these classical models, Hitler could draw on Frederick the Great and especially Richard Wagner, with all his crew of heroes besotted with downfall.

===== Speer said that what he called Hitler's magic was crucially bound up with his nicer aspects, his charm and easy-going warmth, which at least in the 1930s he displayed in his dealings with architects, actors, singers and especially film stars. 'In this way he won me over again and again, particularly after our occasional differences of opinion.'

The dominant picture of Hitler today is therefore completely distorted, he said. It derives mainly from the last few years of the war and represents him as a demonic monster. 'It has been put around – to cover up their own weakness - by the very people who, to put it colloquially, are shitting themselves with fear.' In reality, Hitler was a mixture of energy and eerie enchantment. Of course, Speer also sensed the enormous strength of will peculiar to Hitler, and often enough gave way to it. But for a long time his 'winning and even captivating traits' were there in the background – the Viennese lacquer, as it were, beneath which he concealed his cynically inhuman features. It was with this more than any other quality that he 'hunted Speer down'. Sometimes, when he reads the memoirs of military people and other leaders, he wonders whether he was the only one Hitler 'seduced' in this way.

====== Once more on the 'false' picture of Hitler. In the Führer's headquarters, too, Hitler for most of the time tried to live up to his image as a great statesman with the corresponding dignity and aplomb. No doubt this cost him a considerable effort. For the life he led after the beginning of the war, with its constant train of meetings, large-scale and small-scale 'situation reports', dictations, paper work, and the endless pressure of appointments, was completely opposed to his character and his previous habits in life. The 'periods of inertia', the 'old blankness' that he liked so much, were no longer possible, and presumably the change had caused him quite a lot of trouble. In any event, Speer always admired the energy and extraordinary self-discipline with which Hitler at that time subjected himself to the daily round of duties. In relation to the rapid onset of nervous crises, but also when his dependence on Morell's drugs became apparent, Speer wondered how much each of these owed to the permanent stress and strain.

═══ Speer spoke about a meal at the Munich Vier Jahreszeiten hotel that he attended in 1938 with Hitler, members of the Berghof company and some top Party people. At the end, when they were already getting ready to leave, Hitler took an envelope from his inside breast pocket and presented it in a rather business-like way to Eva Braun as he passed by her (or perhaps he got someone else to present it to her, Speer could no longer remember exactly). Later it was said that the envelope had contained a sum of money.

Speer is still frankly horrified by the incident. Hitler could not have expressed more openly the scant regard he had for the woman who visibly loved him with total commitment, especially as his behaviour conflicted with the somewhat exaggerated Viennese manner that he always observed in relation to women in particular. What he did then, Speer added, was more in keeping with the behaviour familiar from 'American gangster movies'.

We asked him whether all the persecution and harassment, which could not have escaped his ears, had not struck him as morally far more repugnant. He tried this or that answer, but contradicted himself and ended up seeming rather at a loss. Finally he said that he would have to allow our objection in relation to himself, that we had already discussed the topic a few times, and that he had often thought about it since then. At the time in question he had really been convinced that morality was not applicable in politics, and that anyway he was not competent to judge.

We urged him to include the event in the manuscript, as it was a significant example. He agreed with some hesitation. When Speer had gone and we were alone, Siedler said that he had no great hopes. Speer had again had no plausible answer, and in such cases – as we had already observed from time to time – he usually preferred to keep quiet. We spoke about his evident willingness to accept his guilt and his simultaneous inability to come to terms with it analytically.

===== May 1968. Speer told us that, after the Munich conference in 1938, Hitler was in a bad mood for many days and, contrary to habit, vented his anger in petty matters. Of course, no one dared ask him for the reasons, and he himself said nothing. Consequently, he was often happy to stay away from company for days on end because of the reconstruction of the Reich Chancellery. But it may also be the case that he did not take his inner circle seriously enough, especially as everyone considered the outcome of the conference as a great political triumph for the Reich.

It gradually leaked out that, because of the softness of the other powers, Hitler felt he had been swindled out of a real victory. A fortnight later he said at a small gathering that he had been cheated, and not only by the cowardice of the British and French. Another reason why he had not been able to unleash the great conflict was that it would have gone against the mood among his own people. The vacillating Germans had allowed themselves to be unceremoniously duped. 'Our dear Germans!' he added bitterly. 'By that Chamberlain of all people!'

Hitler had concluded by saying that he hoped another such opportunity would present itself. Everything now had to be thrown into working on the public. Countless things still had to be done to instil in it a mood of extreme determination. That was the lesson of Munich.

===== Speer admitted that in autumn 1939 he was among those who said 'yes' to war. But, of course, Hitler never asked him for his opinion. 'Politically I counted for nothing!' he said.

We strongly advised him to include this admission in the text. He asked why we thought it important, since his views had been of no importance at all. We both emphasized that it was important, because it said a lot about the radical nature of his views at the time, even if that was not really like him. In the end he gave way. The few lines that he then managed to include struck both of us as rather meagre, but at least they are there.

━━━━ As Speer admitted under our questioning, despite the cloudy spell after his speech in Poznań in autumn 1943, Hitler's power over him remained undiminished until their meeting in Klessheim in the spring of 1944. Then, because of one or another disagreement in the course of daily business, quite a long period passed in which he saw Hitler either not at all or only for routine official discussions. This estrangement gradually deepened, as these things do, without any active input on either side.

Speer, for his part, was angry and disappointed mainly because of Hitler's behaviour during his illness in mid-January 1944, when he was admitted to the SS hospital at Hohenlychen with a swelling of the knee and a physical as well as probably a nervous breakdown. After that, he considered that it was in Hitler's character to be disloyal. In March Hitler visited Klessheim, near Salzburg, and they saw each other again after a long time. But when he began to speak and again 'tried to draw his cocoon threads around me', he sensed for the first time that his efforts were in vain. Hitler spoke as if from a great distance.

━━━━ The first major difference of opinion with Hitler, before Klessheim and many other occasions, occurred because of Giesler. He felt it as a deliberate slight that Hitler entrusted the 'rival, who was no rival', with the general planning for his native city of Linz. Then came the quarrel with Bormann, who presented himself as an 'honest broker' but who in reality – because he regarded Speer as a competitor for Hitler's favour – furthered Giesler's cause. Speer gave up in response and offered to resign all his posts. He does not deny that Hitler's decision had deeply wounded him, especially as he was unable to give any reason for it. Only later did it become clear to him that it had been a question of a hurtful mood (if there is such a thing) on Hitler's part. In making him uneasy, Hitler had wanted to show that he was the one who set the tone in their relationship.

When we asked Speer whether he had been jealous of Giesler, he flared up: 'For God's sake! Not jealous! But first this or that bit of preferential treatment, then Linz and finally the invitation to accompany us through France to Paris after the victory: it went too far! Giesler was an architect like a hundred others. Besides, he was a terrible petty bourgeois, one of those I have always kept a distance from. How could he oust me in Hitler's favour?' He joked with Wolters and other colleagues that Giesler lived in the 'Dämmergrund'.

'No, no!' Speer continued. Hitler thought of Giesler as merely useful. Significantly, a personal relationship never developed between the two of them. For, precisely in the realm of architecture, Hitler put far greater trust in upper-middle-class people and their stylistic self-assurance: Troost, Todt and himself. But it disturbed him that, early in 1945, he got Giesler to bring a large wooden model of what was planned for Linz to the Reich Chancellery in Berlin. Speer often passed it there in March and once observed Hitler sitting gloomily before it – alone.

Later at Siedler's: about whether he had sensed Speer's annoyance as clearly as I had. With every word he had betrayed the very jealousy he sought to deny.

‗‗‗‗ Speer said that sometime in 1940 Stalin got a middleman to find out whether Hitler would allow him to make a trip to Moscow. Stalin was interested in personally meeting the 'Architect of the Reich', as he was known. He was supposed to have said that Speer's 'triumphal arch' had put in the shade the Soviet pavilion in Paris, and that perhaps a meeting would be useful and instructive for both sides. From what they already knew of Speer's work, people in Moscow found it remarkable and impressive.

'When I told Hitler of this', Speer continued, 'he at first seemed really dumbfounded and close to a fit of rage.' But he soon regained his composure and even grew amused, although an angry tone remained in everything he said. Hitler: Stalin wanted to stick him (Speer) in a 'rat hole', that's the custom there, and not let him go until the new Moscow had been built. But his contract was to build the new capital of the Reich, not the new Moscow.

Whether or not Hitler took seriously Stalin's request or was at least flattered by it, it seemed to prey on his mind. Speer tried not to find out by asking a direct question, but over the next period he alluded several times to Stalin's invitation. He sensed how much Hitler would have liked to know his reaction. But he derived pleasure from leaving Hitler in the dark.

—— Later. Mussolini too had been very interested in his plans for Berlin and had got him to talk about them during his visit to Germany. He said that he would be happy to see him in Rome, to learn more about his ideas on architecture. He would like to put him in contact with his architects, who, as Speer knew, were reckoned among the avant-garde of the new architecture.

—— Speer told us of Hitler's reaction when he drew the buildings of the Third Reich as they would look when they started to collapse centuries later, and when he subsequently set out his so-called theory of ruin value.[2] He certainly did not reckon on the fit of rage that everyone else predicted, but he was prepared to find Hitler quite unreceptive. Against all expectation, however, Hitler became reflective and, after a long silence, mused: 'Yes, great buildings can hold up the march of time!'

I asked Speer whether, in the course of their discussion, he had told Hitler that his remark was quite inappropriate, since both the theory and the drawing he had made demonstrated precisely the superior strength of time. But Speer said that neither the occasion nor the moment had been suitable for that, especially as he was feeling rather unsure of himself. Hitler had been to see Mussolini, who could not have gained acceptance of his great programme for the rebirth of Italy if the buildings of Rome had not been there all around for every Italian to see. For that reason, too, the most important state buildings of the Reich had to be executed in granite.

===== Today, in one of his more talkative moods, Speer said that at the 'height' of his work on forging and drafting plans, when his friendship with Hitler was also strongest despite all the pressure weighing on him, he had occasionally thought that he was becoming a 'second Schinkel'.[3] At the same time, he had been convinced that he would take things further than his great predecessor. For Schinkel had to contend with endless difficulties: shortage of funds, spatial restriction, the stylistic inconsistencies of the epoch, and on top of everything a surly and taciturn king. By contrast, Speer had all the money in the world available to him, encountered no technical or legal obstacles, and had an enthusiastic client in Hitler. Gripped by the general confidence that communicated itself to everyone through the regime, he sometimes asked himself what could possibly go wrong. (He failed to hear, or acted as if he did not hear, my interjection: 'Maybe everything, for that very reason!') And, although he did not become a second Schinkel – he added later – he would anyway go down in the history of architecture. He had been pretty confident in himself, sharing the arrogance that 'filled and deceived us all'. This he said somewhat shamefully, as if he were laying bare his most secret thoughts.

═══ Today to Siedler: I have a feeling that Speer 'demonizes' himself too much. The comparison with Faust and Mephistopheles, which he draws at the beginning of the manuscript, strikes me as greatly exaggerated and somewhat redolent of petty-bourgeois educational kitsch. I recommended deleting the passage.

But Siedler replied that it is evidently important to Speer: he is precisely given to melodrama and will not give it up. I said something about the dreadful German penchant for 'Ecce homo' attitudes.

═══ Speer: 'With the start of the Russian campaign in 1941, I was increasingly beset with doubts that Berlin, my most important life's work, would ever be completed. When I hinted at my concern to Hitler – in an extremely oblique way, of course – he reacted almost angrily and insisted that all the completion deadlines must be met: 1945, 1950, and so on. I saw this as just another sign of his unease and a tendency to want to have everything at once: victory and the monuments immediately afterwards. With a sense of our importance, we in the inner circle of the General Inspectorate of Buildings (Liebel, Hettlage, Wolters and myself) sometimes joked that Hitler was waging his campaigns not least so that he could place contracts for triumphal arches.'

After he became a minister, the idea sometimes crept up on him that he would never be able to return to the

architectural profession. He also caught himself thinking of
Berlin as 'my beautiful ghost town'.

===== Hitler's remarkable awkwardness with so-called
experts. It was as if his irritating self-opinionatedness evapor-
ated when he faced a combination of specialist knowledge
and a strong personality, and sometimes experts could obtain
what no minister was capable of pushing through. The only
exception was generals, whom Hitler obviously did not
regard as experts.

He himself was the exception in the other sense, Speer
assured us. Almost always Hitler was faintly inhibited or
'half-sure' in relation to him. 'Speer, I underwrite everything
that you come up with', he used to say, and Speer made no
new friends as a result. Things were already like that in their
discussions about planning for Berlin (not so much Nuremberg) and above all during his time as a minister.

A first change came with the appearance of Fritz Sauckel,
the General Plenipotentiary for the Employment of Labour;
Hitler often backed Sauckel against him, for whatever
reason. And then, of course, in the dispute with the gauleiters and over the Nero instruction.[4] But a residual awkwardness on Hitler's side remained even at the end, especially
when there were sharp clashes after days of a kind of reconciliation. It was nearly always Hitler who started it. Speer
can still remember his insecure, 'canvassing' laughter, as it
were, whenever he wanted to restore harmony between
them. And perhaps this 'insecurity' (or whatever one likes to
call it), from which Hitler never managed to free himself,
was ultimately what saved his life when he admitted defiance
of his orders.

4

THE MINISTER: FLYING STARTS AND

STUMBLING BLOCKS

Sylt, August 1968. When Hitler unexpectedly appeared in Rastenberg on 7 February 1942, Speer was initially taken aback that, contrary to his habits, he did not even find time to receive him briefly. He was told that Minister Todt was with the Führer, and in the restaurant to which he went after his arrival it was even said that things were 'pretty lively' in the Führer's building. There had already been talk on various occasions about differences between Hitler and Dr Todt following the disastrous winter. But, given the admiration that Hitler felt for Todt, no one thought it possible that there would be a vociferous dispute between them, possibly ending in the minister's resignation. In late 1941, in a private conversation at his little house near Berchtesgaden, Todt explained to Speer that the lost battle in the winter had shown Hitler's whole strategic conception to be mistaken. Now it was the statesman's hour, so to speak. It was time to end the war politically. He had also let Hitler know this.

Thus, when Todt died in a plane crash at take-off the next morning, there was a suspicion that he had been assassinated. At first Speer too thought this likely, and even Hitler seemed suspicious. Consequently, he is convinced to this day that Hitler had no knowledge of an attempt on Todt's life, still less that he ordered it. On the other hand, SS Reichsführer Heinrich Himmler may have had reasons of his own to want Todt out of the way: after all, if anything were to have happened to Hitler, he would have had to build Todt into his calculations. But, on closer examination, it was out of the question that Himmler could have been behind a murder attempt. Speer is convinced that Himmler was then still too dependent on Hitler. The same was true of people in his upper ranks, including Heydrich.

It should also be borne in mind, Speer continued, that in the event of a power struggle the SS had nothing to fear from Dr Todt, since he did not have a power base of his own. He had always been a loner. But – Speer interrupted himself – it was difficult for him to take a position on this set of issues. As is well known, he himself was suspected of being one of the masterminds behind a possible assassination.

To the point that he was indeed the only person in Hitler's entourage who might have had an interest in Dr Todt's removal, he replied heatedly that that was 'complete nonsense'. At that time he did not count at all politically; even Todt described him to others as 'politically naïve'. Above all, however, he saw himself purely as an architect. Admittedly he wanted to make a contribution to victory, but he never thought of switching to a completely different field of activity. Anyway, all the accusations against him were raised only after the war, especially by the circle around Todt's family.

══════ When Hitler called him in at midday on 8 February, it was clear that he would have to take on some of Todt's

8 February 1942: immediately after his appointment as Reich Minister for Arms and Munitions, Speer appears before his staff in heavy snow in the ministry courtyard.

construction duties. Hitler behaved very officially, standing in the middle of the room and avoiding the informal style that had developed between them. After his expression of condolences, Hitler pulled himself up straight, as if to make him aware of the solemnity of the occasion, and then without more ado appointed him as successor to all of Todt's posts. He, Speer, muttered something about the unique construction duties, the effort he would make to be a worthy successor to the great man who was now gone, and so on. But Hitler interrupted him with unusual energy, repeated the formula of appointment and added: 'It's a question of the whole job! You'll manage it! You have my trust, and if there are problems let me know about them.' Hitler was suddenly the complete Führer, very firm, as if there was no personal-collegial relationship between them.

At that moment he had one of the best, but certainly also the most useful, ideas in his life. He asked Hitler, as a kind of service in return, for nothing less than a promise of unconditional support. At first he expected that Hitler would not go that far. But, after a moment of hesitation, in which he presumably weighed up the consequences at lightning speed, he accepted everything. 'You have my word', he assured him.

====== I asked Speer what led to the astonishing decision to make him armaments minister – a man whom Hitler on occasions described as an 'unworldly' artist. He was master of a huge, Europe-wide apparatus, boss of countless production plants, a kind of commander over a maze of industrial sites each with clearly demarcated responsibilities yet cooperating precisely together – all of which made him more 'worldly' than anyone else. And so forth.

Speer replied that for a long time he thought it was one of Hitler's whims of friendship. In the rather cold world of the Führer's headquarters, Hitler sensed for the first time the ever greater isolation in which he was caught up, and so he wanted to have people around who were close to him. I objected that perhaps another consideration was that Speer had proved a highly talented organizer in 1938 during the construction of the new Reich Chancellery, as the rapid completion of the building work had been a far more masterly achievement than the actual architecture.

With some hesitation Speer agreed. Of course, the completion of the Reich Chancellery was not sufficient proof of his capability for the extremely difficult post of armaments minister. But that 'talent test' may have played a part, even if he still thinks that Hitler's mood played a decisive role, as it nearly always did in his personnel decisions.

===== To the question whether, in their night talk on 7–8 February 1942, Hitler had rejected Todt's suggestion that they [Todt and Speer] fly back together from Rastenberg to Berlin, Speer replied that he had already been asked that by some fellow prisoners in Nuremberg and then Spandau. But, however much he tries, he is unable to remember. In so far as this contains the other question about whether Hitler knew of an attempt on Todt's life, he must again answer in the negative. Despite everything we now know, he does not think that Hitler was capable of such 'cold-blooded vileness'. Hitler not only knew and respected Todt; he also needed him. Speer dismissed a reference to Röhm by saying: 'But he feared Röhm and his million-strong SA. Not Todt.'

'But', I interjected, 'perhaps he feared the mood of pessimism that Todt might have spread.' Speer looked pensive for a moment. Then: 'It comes down to what one thinks was possible. And I say: no. But, after all we now know, I can't rule it out.'

===== After his appointment as minister, he probably made his first appearance too early before the Party authorities (a good two weeks later). But he knew what significance they would attach to it, including for his own activity. Already in the first few days, there was vociferous criticism when his plans for industry to assume 'independent responsibility' became known. It was said that he could not free himself of his bourgeois origin, that he was 'industry's man'. In his impetuosity he wanted to take the bull by the horns, especially as everyone recommended the old platitude about dealing with the 'crude stuff' right at the beginning. Moreover, the importance of his new position of power had filled him with great self-assurance, and Hitler's promise of support had added one more element.

'But it was a beginner's mistake', he added, shaking his head, as if amazed at his naïve impracticality.

═════ Surprisingly, Speer said today that he spent many too many years of his life on things that diverged from, and in part even contradicted, his own aims and preferences. He wonders how this came about. Perhaps it was ambition, perhaps weakness, or perhaps also a need to excel in fields that were actually alien to him. But the question is what a man of his ambition and desire for effect should have preferred.

═════ On Speer's original rule that no leading colleague should be more than fifty-five years old, and that deputies should at most be forty. In this way he made the staff exceptionally youthful, and soon people were using the expression 'Speer's boys' and speaking of the 'knavish pranks' they permitted themselves. Speer: 'No one past his mid-fifties who has been successful escapes the proven formula. Everything turns into routine and arrogance.'

═════ It was a mad period, Speer said today. Already in his years as an architect he lived in a kind of intoxication, as a man constantly possessed. Only when everything was over did he ask himself whether there had not also been an element of escapism in his mania for work. But escape from what? we threw in. Especially as he knew nothing of the crimes? Perhaps escape from the world of politics, an alien world for him with its thousand intrigues, ambushes and traps. But even today, Speer replied, he cannot be more precise. Anyway, who ever knows what is driving them? Saints and philosophers perhaps, but they are not really 'driven'. If they were, they would not be saints or philosophers.

Recently, he once tried to reconstruct a random day. He had seventeen important appointments, not including the routine ones. Sometimes there may have been twenty appointments, but never fewer than fifteen. It never happened that he went to bed before midnight, and he often felt 'almost dead' as he fell asleep. It really had been 'a kind of death' in which he lived then, if one can put it like that.

═══ I took up Speer's earlier point that, after his appointment as minister, he increasingly doubted whether Berlin-Germania would ever be completed. He said that for a long time he had talked himself into believing that the whole project would be accomplished. For, as always with such mega-projects, there was a fair degree of giddiness in the enthusiasm that filled him and his colleagues. Today he has known for a long time that they were fooling themselves, but also that that kind of fever is one of the worst temptations which artists, and naturally architects, have to face. Those who are unable to remain cool should steer clear of art. He kept repeating this, as the fundamental insight he had gained from life.

I went on to ask Speer how long Hitler had believed in the realization of his world capital 'Germania'. He replied that Hitler never completely gave up the idea. 'He was a real somnambulist.' But his craziest dreams had come true too often, and so he thought that this time too the 'lucky star' about which he sometimes spoke would carry him forward, so long as he pursued his goal with the utmost vigour. 'I once called that his "magic table" hope.'

But – Speer said a little later – in February or March 1945, in response to something about the transformation and beautification of German cities, Hitler answered out of the blue: 'Ah, Speer, drop that! It was all fantasy.' It was a long time since he had watched those buildings and streets taking shape. He did sometimes have the plans brought to him. The reason was simple: he needed that! He had to be able to paint the world for himself – or at least a part of it. 'I can't cope just with reality.'

===== In this connection I asked Speer whether for Hitler construction plans had been a kind of compensation for his destruction mania. But he rejected this almost indignantly. True, Hitler had a kind of destruction compulsion, but it was never unqualified. He destroyed what set itself up against him; he knew no limits in that respect. But it was one of my 'psychological imaginings' that he wrecked things for the sake of it, like a child breaking his toy.

===== This morning, when he reported the fruits of his night-time deliberation, Speer said in an unusually declamatory tone: In the inner circle of such a system, the faculty of perception is greatly reduced. There is a kind of 'inner blindness', which is reinforced by the need to repress all manner of things.

===== Sylt, September 1968. On Hitler's tendency to foster rivalries. Speer said it was less an expression of his 'divide et impera' principle than a result of his 'struggle for existence' doctrine. The two together led directly to a chaos of competing responsibilities and the endless disputes associated with it. Already in the Berghof days a scornful rumour had it that Hitler had given both Heinrich Hoffmann and others unlimited authority to make competing bids at auctions. His view was that the strongest would then win the bid – which explains the exorbitant prices paid for paintings by Spitzweg, Grützner and others. 'But, of course, it was only a funny story that someone had thought up, though I laughed at it like everyone else. Hitler was no fool.'

===== We concluded from various remarks of Speer's that he still felt a certain pride at having been described as

Hitler's 'second man' and perhaps presumed successor. Today I asked him once more whether he seriously thought he had been in the reckoning, and he answered after only a moment's hesitation: 'Yes. Of course!' I mentioned the powerful line-up on the other side: Himmler, Goebbels, Bormann, Goering and many others.

This time Speer took longer to reply and began by pointing out that during his lifetime Hitler's decision would have been generally accepted, and that even after his death it would have had absolute validity; everyone would undoubtedly have attached the highest authority to the word of the deceased Führer. I should also bear in mind that Speer's opponents, however powerful they may have been, were at loggerheads with one another, and that he would naturally have had to enter into temporary coalitions; at any rate the loyal Wehrmacht, which was used to taking orders, supported him. To this I asked whether he had really had 'the' Wehrmacht behind him, or only some desk generals well known for their vacillation and opportunism. But he did not accept my objection. Besides, he said, his only serious rival had been Himmler, but he – as the shadowy master of the SS, the police and the concentration camps and prison system – would certainly have had a hard time against him. 'I was nothing if not popular with the public', he added with unusual self-assurance.

More time on this, and Speer said that of course the outcome was highly uncertain, as always in a power struggle. 'But I was not without my chances.' That evening, Siedler and I were both surprised that the question was clearly preoccupying Speer more than he ever admitted. The futility of his strategic considerations is evident in the fact that his own fall began at the moment when Hitler first named him as a possible candidate for the succession – nor is there even agreement about how seriously Hitler had meant it.

═══ Today, one day later, I asked Speer about the seriousness of Hitler's remark about the succession. I wanted to know whether Hitler had ever said with any binding force that he at least belonged to the inner circle of candidates. Speer replied that there had been only hints, mostly in the form of disparaging remarks about those who belonged to the shortlist: Goering, Goebbels, Himmler, Hess, and especially Bormann. One was too idle and vain, another had a crippled foot, another had too little feeling for art, or was too narrow-minded, and so on. Anyway, once or twice Hitler did give him to understand that Goering had for the longest time been the successor Führer, and that he, Speer, had the best prospects of taking Goering's place. But then, usually a couple of sentences later, a remark that placed everything in doubt.

After a brief pause for thought, Speer said that this had been due not only to Hitler's indecisiveness but also to his 'tactical guile'. He came away wondering whether Hitler had not been playing one of his games. Perhaps what spoke most in his favour was the fact that Hitler seemed unable to settle on anyone else as his successor.

═══ Speer said that things had been very easy with Goering, easier than with anyone else. The recipe was always the same. One had to take into account his laziness and his pride, and then he unfailingly gave way. For the substance of the matter did not concern him, only the figure that he cut. In conclusion, Speer said that in no one else from the top leadership whom he knew reasonably well was he as disappointed as he was in Goering. When he took ministerial office, he had thought of him as the strongest of his partners or opponents. But he was the weakest, and after a few weeks he seemed no longer an opponent but just a kind of puppet grumbling as he danced 'on my strings'.

===== I asked Speer about the forced labour, which was not the least of the reasons why he was sentenced. He said that, whenever he learned of inhuman conditions, he did the best he could, however little it may have been, to put things right or to make them better. But, I persisted, many tens of thousands met their death, often in appalling circumstances.

We walked silently side by side for a while near Munkmarsch. Then Speer said that the deaths of so many people weighed on his mind. Right at the beginning, before the tribunal and during the first few years in Spandau, he tried to calm himself with the thought that, in the prevailing 'chaos', forced labourers were the formal responsibility of Sauckel, partly of Himmler and in the end, like everything else, of Hitler. But such comforts soon came to an end in the face of a cell wall. This accounts for his recognition of the Nuremberg Tribunal and acceptance of the victors' verdict, as well as the fact that he defended himself again and again before his fellow prisoners. 'What else would explain it?' he added, after a brief pause.

So, he concluded, he does not need anyone to tell him how terrible things were in many camps and what a burden of responsibility falls on him and all the others. He would like to say, however, that conditions were not always as horrific as it has repeatedly been claimed since Nuremberg. He mentioned several factories and some of the things he saw by chance there, then turned to the agricultural operations, where things were reasonably okay for forced labourers, and so on. When I contradicted him, he referred to the male nurse Toni Proost, who a few days after his arrival in Spandau offered to carry secret messages for him, to express a kind of gratitude for the good treatment he had received as a forced labourer, including medical care during a serious illness. Speer insisted that he did not want to gloss over anything, but it also had to be said that one of the consequences of such a terrible war was that, with the growing distance in time, heroic acts on one side and sufferings on the other assumed ever greater dimensions.

To the further question whether his efforts to ensure reasonably tolerable conditions stemmed from humanitarian considerations or from a wish to increase productivity, Speer said that in war on such a scale any motive would be eroded by something like the 'efficiency mania' overshadowing everything else. It was precisely a kind of 'fury', which 'gripped each one of us'.

Later he took up the theme again. Things had not been completely different on the other side. There too, as we now know, the rules were violated again and again in the treatment of war prisoners and other cases – by the Russians, that goes without saying, but to a considerable extent also by the French, the Americans and others. There were different degrees of violation, of course. But the principle that still applied in the Geneva or Hague Convention and elsewhere did not count for very much on either side.

===== Heidelberg, November 1968. Discussion of the manuscript as a whole, its merits and shortcomings. We again asked Speer to give more personal details: that was the area of greatest weakness. But he countered that he had shown himself as he was; maybe we were asking for a Speer that he was unable to provide.

To make things more specific, Siedler asked how Speer would have acted if at some point – in 1941, for example – he had received irrefutable proof of the crimes in the East. Would he have approached Hitler? Would he have given up his building plans? Made representations to Bormann? Informed generals and close colleagues whom he trusted? Or, at least, his friend and Hitler's personal physician, Dr Brandt? Speer seemed confused for a moment and said:

April 1942: Hitler, Speer and Hermann Goering inspect new weapons. On the left is Heinrich Hoffmann, while behind Hitler and Speer is Erich Raeder.

'No, I don't think so.' Then: 'Despite any evidence, I simply wouldn't have believed such reports of atrocities.'

══════ In the afternoon we pressed Speer again. He was visibly suffering. But Siedler and I had agreed beforehand that, although the existing manuscript contained many general condemnations and confessions of guilt, it was still colourless and filled with empty words.

If one tried to summarize the several hours of discussion, Speer's argument in self-justification was roughly as follows. Of course, by the latest at the start of the war, or soon after, he suspected that the regime had a 'dark side'. From time to time things came to his ears which, if he had asked further questions, would certainly have led him to draw terrible conclusions. The problem was precisely that he did not ask further questions. In this connection, he again mentioned the episode with the Breslau gauleiter Karl Hanke, who told him allusively of the horrifying conditions in a camp in Upper Silesia, by which he obviously meant Auschwitz.

———— Speer said that one of the 'truly evil aspects' of a regime like Hitler's was precisely its ability to prevent such thoughts and to make people afraid of their likely consequences. Like everyone, he developed a great ability to close his eyes and ears. Today he is not even sure whether he closed them deliberately or just let the outrages pass him by without thinking of them.

We objected that everything he said contained precisely the kind of generalities that are so unsatisfactory; the whole manuscript lacked tangible material about the strictly personal dimension. As counter-evidence, he mentioned the account of his visit to the Mittelwerk ('Dora'). The conditions he found there really startled him, and he has also described the action he took to improve them, however much SS Brigadier Kammler and the head of the so-called Labour Front, Ley, tried to obstruct him.

But, he added, it did not occur to him to question the whole regime and the role he played in it. Still, he must say that the images from the dungeons haunted him for a long time – although he knows that that is a feeble defence, or no defence at all. At the end of our discussion, which had taken place in an unusually tense atmosphere, he entirely dispelled our critical mood by saying with an inimitable gesture of sincerity: 'The answer to the question of why I loyally went on serving a regime that not only permitted but organized such horror is what I have been trying to find for years.'

———— Later in the evening. We are not convinced. We think that Speer's evasiveness, together with his playing at hide and seek against 'a backdrop of innocence' (as Siedler summed it up), offers a target in the book that is totally unnecessary and may lead to unpleasant as well as misguided reactions. I hinted that I would find it hard really to get involved in it, especially as, with regard to my original aim of obtaining informative eye-witness material about Hitler, I had so far been given a lot that was atmospherically very important but less that was factually revealing than I had hoped. Siedler kept things calm by acting as if he had not heard what I said.

We then recalled that Speer had not so much as mentioned the pogrom night of November 1938. I said that the reader would find this impossible to understand, and we agreed to extract at least some statement from him. Surely he must have found it horrifying to be faced with an act of open civil war, so to speak, on the part of the state or the state-party, in peacetime in a civilized country. What did he observe? What did he feel and think? What conclusions did he draw? Evidently none. But he must give some explanation for that. And so on, and so forth. We decided to remain intransigent and even to risk a crisis.

===== Before we parted Siedler and I, as often recently, returned to the question of what Speer had known of the mass crimes. We believed his constant protestations as little as his defence counsel at Nuremberg, Dr Flächsner, and almost everyone else had done. Too many pieces of circumstantial evidence suggest otherwise, and straight off we will adduce more than a dozen. But we are also aware that they are no more than circumstantial. Up to now there is no proof. We know too that, even in honest people, the power of repression is far greater than anyone thinks possible.

===== When we met after breakfast this morning, Speer appeared almost jovial, although we could tell he was making an effort to get over the tensions and even hidden moods of the previous day. On the walk that Siedler invited us to take with the remark that nature was propitious, it was my job to make the opening move. At once the agitation that seemed to have died down was there again; Speer was almost desperate, with a kind of 'pleading' look in his eyes. At some point, he told us, he had reconstructed that on the morning after the pogrom of 9 November 1938 he must have passed by the synagogue on Fasanenstrasse, or at any rate that it lay in his path. But he assured us again that with the best will in the world he could not say anything about it. Essentially what we were demanding was to link the answer to the 'cardinal question' of his life with an event about which he had not retained a single memory. That was a gross error from a technical-authorial point of view, and he could not understand why we did not see that.

Siedler turned on all his charm, but he pursued the matter with uncharacteristic obstinacy. He said it would be very informative to know why Speer's humanity, his conscience, one might also say his civic instincts, did not rebel at the sight of the synagogue ruins, which he described as still smouldering. Since the mass of people reacted in the same way, his own account would be of the utmost significance. The very fact that the event left him so indifferent makes his case representative, and so on.

There followed an almost dogged argument about the matter. Speer stubborn, now and then hot-tempered, as we had never seen him before. For the first time I got a sense of the other Speer, the one behind the shy and up to now even bashful appearance: a man of energy and great self-assertiveness. At one point it occurred to me that he had slipped back into his old discarded skin. As a minister, he must have liked to veer around like that with his people, although of course he observed the forms and was still forced to retain a 'cultivated' self-control. Eventually we ended the discussion without any results. But I said to Siedler that now the crisis had begun, and I pondered how and whether we could continue working together.

═══ Stutenhof, January 1969. Once more the tiresome subject. Meanwhile Speer appears to have regained his composure; he also looks less stressed than he did recently. He mentioned our quarrel without great trouble: two weeks earlier we had spoken to one another in much too much of a 'rage'; at that time, though, we evidently had a problem to solve, and in such situations one should advance as soon as possible with an extremely cool head.

A walk on the Watt.[1] The difficulty for him, Speer began, is that he no longer understands the person he used to be, and yet it is that person who is always at issue. Siedler took up the thread and spoke of his understanding for Speer's distress ('respect and' – as he knows – 'a sympathy stretching far into the human side of things'), for the peculiar obstacles in the way of his attempt to reduce the two lives he led to a common denominator, and for his irritation at the constant tension he has to endure because of the preoccupation with the past. But not only had all of us resolved to make it intelligible to today's reader; the book should also have a lasting existence as a historical document. And more of this fine, persuasive stuff.

But, I persisted, it was important to deal with the pogrom night and (as I now learned) the morning after. It was a question of the only concrete admission of error reaching into the personal dimension of things, and after careful consideration I was not prepared to leave it out. He should regard that as a final word, so to speak. All we were asking of him was a few pages, in which he would describe what he experienced and why those events, like other arbitrary acts of the

regime, left him so unaffected. Was it coldness, indifference
or cowering in a regime of terror? Perhaps he had also felt
himself to be unconditionally on the side of the 'terrorists'?
Speer looked annoyed and visibly taken aback. After some
toing and froing, in the course of which Siedler skilfully
trimmed our impudence without abandoning our actual
request, Speer finally gave in. As we parted, he told us that
he would immediately get to work on it.

══════ From many comments made in public, Speer said, he
gathers that there are considerable difficulties in understanding why he tried to boost the war effort for so long, even
beyond the point at which victory had been irrevocably gam-
bled away.

It was not just blindness, he assured us. Rather, he had
hopes in some political solution that might occur to Hitler,
especially as he often consoled his entourage with such a
prospect: a special peace perhaps, the break-up of the enemy
coalition that he had been trying to promote, or something
like that. Anyway, Hitler repeatedly had an inspiration in
critical situations – above all when he had his back to the
wall. Why not again this time? Hitler once explained to him
that an acceptable solution could be achieved only from a
position of strength, such as came only through the utmost
mobilization of one's forces. He had to gain time; it was all
just a struggle for 'a paltry bit of time'. Later Speer would
hear this phrase from him over and over again.

Therefore, Speer continued, he allied himself with
Goebbels in the policy of 'total war' and continued throughout to step up the arms effort. Only right at the end, and
even then only with many fluctuations, did he realize that
Hitler was striving not for some interim success but for
nothing other than the country's downfall. This insight was
the decisive reason for his decision to defy the 'scorched

June 1944: Speer displays the growth of German weapons production to managers in the arms industry.

earth' policy. But, despite many prior apprehensions, he did not perceive this earlier than the autumn of 1944, especially as Hitler, both in the above-mentioned conversation and on another occasion, variously alluded to the fact that some (never specified) measures were imminent.

===== Only after a long time, and at the earliest by the beginning of 1943, did he become aware of Hitler's growing uncertainty. He still believes that, if Hitler had been as decisive as in the 1930s, the war would have taken a different course, and that at least a political solution could have been achieved at the right time.

By then, however, Hitler was continually wavering and oscillating and going back on decisions. Speer himself quite often evaded the resulting difficulties by deciding on his own initiative what should be done, without reference to the

proper chain of command. Others, especially the SS, did the
same. In any event, Hitler drove everyone to despair. The
visible chaos in the executive should in no small part be
attributed to this. Autumn 1943 brought the first open clash,
when Hitler behaved towards him as he had previously done
only with pig-headed generals. From then on, for this reason
too (as already explained in various ways), he often thought
of withdrawing from the whole oppressive world of politics.

—— He had been in agreement with Goebbels that Hitler
made a grave mistake by beginning to shun the public during
the war. Not only because of the mood in the population,
but because appearances before the masses always strengthened him and functioned as a kind of elixir of life. After Stalingrad he made no more public appearances, or perhaps just
one. Presumably he feared having to present himself as a
loser and kept waiting for a great victory that would again
allow him 'to go up to people'. But the victory did not come,
and Hitler secretly knew that. Sometimes Speer had the
impression that he no longer believed himself capable even
of making a great speech.

Goebbels therefore to some extent took over the role of
people's tribune, and one aim of his many appearances – in
particular, the famous speech at the Sportspalast in February
1943 – was certainly to stand in for Hitler as a speaker. 'At
that time Goebbels spoke everywhere fairly openly about a
"leader crisis", implying that it was the main reason for our
difficulties.'

—— Speer said that, in two respects, the so-called table
talk was only semi-authentic. He always sensed that Hitler
was making a special effort to show the various guests how
comprehensive was his knowledge and how far it extended to
the remotest detail. He later found himself agreeing with

others who attended these monologues that Hitler expressed himself in an affected manner, as if he were twisting and turning before his listeners. Anyway, the talk that he remembers was expressed much more crudely or primitively, in a more plebeian manner.

But, on these occasions, Hitler was also much more impressive, if one can put it like that, much more persuasive. Of course he knew that his words were being taken down for future generations. This was certainly another reason for him to put on airs before his 'true idol', posterity.

It should also be borne in mind, Speer said, that even Dr Picker, who compiled the shorthand texts for the longest period, did not wish to risk losing the goodwill of his client, Bormann, and therefore did not exactly change Hitler's expositions but presumably smoothed them out with some circumspection. In the innermost circle – which, as the war progressed and especially after the quarrel with the generals, became reduced to his doctors and secretaries plus a few personal adjutants – Hitler controlled himself much less and in the end no longer thought about effects. To be sure, he was also more tired and exhausted, with a visibly diminished stimulus threshold, so that he became upset by any trivial remark.

5

BREAKING WITH HITLER

Heidelberg, late January 1969. Speer said that the turn away from Hitler essentially took place during their meetings in March 1944, or even a few weeks earlier at the Hohenlychen sanatorium. He had stopped off in Klessheim, near Salzburg, on his way to a period of convalescent leave in the South Tirol. Hitler came over to see him and for some time the conversation developed with difficulty, although he exerted all his charm to win him back by asking 'in the Viennese style' after the progress of his recovery, 'the health of your good wife' and the children. Then he summoned up common memories and began to speak of the buildings they would energetically bring to completion once the 'damned war' was over. On armaments issues, however, he did not utter a word throughout their conversation.

Everything was the same as always, Speer continued, and yet quite different. Suddenly the veil was torn, he had thought as Hitler was speaking, and for the first time he caught himself listening with only 'half an ear'. His occasional interjections – 'Ah!' or 'I see' – must have come out sounding rather absent-minded, and his answers quite taciturn. Probably he struck Hitler as somewhat wooden. But, as soon as his unexpected visitor had appeared in the door, he had revealed his ugliness as clearly as if he had simply removed a mask. Never before had Speer noticed his common forehead, his wide nose, the ordinariness of everything about him, or, as Herr Siedler always puts it, his 'little man's features': all the things he has described in the manuscript.

Hitler's ugliness was further emphasized by his pasty skin colour and bloated features. And, as he talked insistently to Speer, it was as if they silently grew further and further apart. He let Hitler sense his reserve; after all, there was no reason why he 'should be spared it'. From time to time he was seized by a 'sense of futility' and asked himself what he was really doing there. Anyway everything was lost: the war as well as the great buildings he had sketched on his drawing table. So, he remained speechless and asked himself what was still left to be said.

In the afternoon of the following day, Hitler appeared with an orderly carrying a huge flower arrangement that almost blotted out the poor man. As this was rather unusual, his first thought was: 'This is farewell. So, this is how it's ending.' To his own surprise, however, the thought that their association was coming to an end scarcely affected or upset him.

Naturally, the decisive reason for his feeling of estrangement was that, as soon as he had been absent for a while because of illness, Hitler had fallen in with the intrigues of Goering and the construction boss, Franz Xavier Dorsch. Now he came and acted as if nothing had happened, as if – Speer added in one of his few successful images – one could switch off a friendship and 'switch it on again' when the occasion arose. He saw this as an expression of disdain from which he had previously thought himself exempt.

Naturally, too, it was not a question of a sudden complete break. Rather, it was a lengthy process, with doubts, relapses and new flare-ups of estrangement. Nevertheless, when Hitler asked him after their final discussion to join the old Berghof party in late April 1944, he went there 'feeling relieved and even happy', despite the still prevailing dreariness and the jokes that were as much of a torture as in the past. After a pause, he said mainly for himself: How can you ever get on the track of someone with such emotional fractures?

As for the rest, Hitler's attitude to him was constantly fluctuating in those days. At the situation reviews, after the first exuberance of reconciliation, he found himself returning to his carping frame of mind; Hitler reproached him several times for constantly hinting at his doubts about victory, and described his memoranda as 'cold and pedantic', lacking the necessary confidence. Then there was Hitler's remark soon after 20 July 1944,[1] when he stated that the German people were doomed to go under if they lost the war. That shook him deeply. He was also dismayed when Hitler put a stop to the harmless little meetings that he sometimes attended with other ministers on the initiative of finance minister Schwerin von Krosigk. Speer thinks that his presence at them prompted Hitler's intervention – not because he was so very important, but because Hitler wanted above all to hurt his feelings.

━━━━━ Schloss Korb, near Merano, February 1969. Speer remarked that Hitler was extremely sensitive in matters to do with obedience and subordination, and everywhere suspected a revolt against his (actually never endangered) authority. Sometimes Speer had wondered whether in his essential character Hitler did not suffer from a deep inferiority complex. One indication of this was his incessant quarrels

Hitler, Speer and (between them) Wilhelm Keitel, inspecting a captured Soviet tank in 1942

with the generals, and anyone who contradicted him or tended to have doubts soon found himself on the retired list.

Thus Speer thinks that, when he tendered his resignation in early 1944, it struck Hitler as a bolt from the blue; Milch spread the rumour that he had spoken of 'almost incredible impertinence'. Again it had been a question of fearing for his authority. Speer, Hitler had said, was naturally wrong in substance, but far worse was the threat he had taken it upon himself to issue. It confirmed all the accusations of Bormann and the gauleiters about his essentially unsympathetic attitude to the Party. A little later, according to Walter Hewel, the link to the foreign ministry, Hitler had been in a more conciliatory mood and referred to his well-known fondness for intelligent outsiders. But he had also said that big problems were to be expected with such people, and that Speer thought of himself too much as an artist above all the rules of obedience; the fact was that at the moment Speer was above all a minister and had to fall into line.

Goering made the same reproach when he called him about his intention to resign. What did he think he was doing? he roared in his usual way. Under the laws of the movement and the National Socialist state, no one had the right simply to stop working for Hitler; anyway Speer did not exactly come from the ranks of the old Party fighters. Goering was his master's voice: Hitler never had authority problems with him, however powerful he looked on the outside.

This was the period when he began to avoid the Führer's headquarters and even Hitler's presence more often and, as he noted with some surprise, more resolutely than he had already been doing since the end of 1943.

===== Speer said today that the head of the British Bomber Command, Sir Arthur Harris, had always struck him as a primitive type in the manner of most generals, narrow-minded and even a little stupid. In fact, he had no strategy at all for the air war, only a killer's tedious cast of mind. Germany had been so extremely vulnerable, Speer continued, but Harris had not seen that. There's the enemy, so keep hitting him with everything you've got! That was his motto.

Of course, the way in which Harris waged the air war was a nightmare for the civilian population. But it allowed him [Speer] to preserve the arms industry from collapse, and when agitated colleagues came and said everything was going to pieces he was able to calm them down. An adversary like Harris was too simple-minded 'really to put us in danger'. When the Americans became actively involved in the air war, he was at first afraid that they would immediately introduce a better thought-out strategy at Combined Operations, and General Spaatz did indeed try to do that. But Harris evidently had strategic 'seniority'. Peculiar, still today.

Speer added that, when the selective bombings, 'as we called them', got under way in 1944, it was soon the end of arms and even of any warfare worthy of the name. A lot about the air war, the enemy's unidentified opportunities, but also the lengthening of the war that was the result. We noted that he and the Allies did everything in conjunction, as it were, to delay the end.

======== Speer said that already at Nuremberg, and later in Spandau, some of his fellow prisoners liked to say in his presence that Sir Arthur Harris should also really be facing a war-crimes tribunal. In any event, the indiscriminate bombing war against a defenceless civilian population was morally no different from Lidice and Oradour and the countless other acts of barbarism committed during the war. The German commander responsible in each case was brought before a court and usually sentenced to death. But Harris received acclaim as well as medals and decorations.

In Spandau, Speer continued, it was mainly Grand Admiral Dönitz and Rudolf Hess who tried to challenge him by asking what the difference was between the famous thousand-bomber attacks and a camp like Theresienstadt, between Dresden and Oradour. However, he never replied to their mostly scornful attacks; he simply walked off and left the questioner standing there. His fellow prisoner Walther Funk, evidently at his wit's end, once called after him: there goes 'Herr Speer, our enemies' well-known floozie'.

Speer said that these attacks really embarrassed him; he never found an answer. And, after thinking about it, he too has come to the view that Harris's rightful place is before a war tribunal. Many others too, and not only on the Soviet side. He never said this to Dönitz and Funk, however, nor does he raise the issue in the existing manuscript. For he thinks it is not up to him to express such comparisons. But, in this respect, the victors once again have the last word. Justice is indeed a 'poor virtue'.

====== I returned once more to Speer's claim that the rightful place for the Allied air war is before a tribunal, if one is to judge its operations by the same strict standards that were applied to the conduct of the Germans. I said that actually he should not argue such things, especially as in 1939, according to his own statement, he belonged to the so-called war party. In a sense, the fleets of bombers brought 'his' war back to Germany.

Speer's reply was unusually astute: 'Just because it was "my" or "our" war which destroyed cities and sometimes hunted down individuals, did this make it permissible for the Allies to wage war in the manner of the Germans? Is that what you mean?' He thought that those who, like Sir Arthur Harris, deliberately waged war against the civilian population should anyway not put on airs and draw upon the morality of a better world. We Germans undoubtedly committed enormous crimes. We were also the first to commit them. But the British and Americans always claimed that they wanted to free the world from evil – instead of which they themselves, without a moment's hesitation, resorted to evil as a means.

Towards the end of the conversation, Speer added that almost the only difference was that our enemies of the day claimed the last word, as they were entitled to do. He said 'almost' because he was aware that he had not taken into account the eradication of so-called inferior races. That made a difference. And, after a pause: that really made an immeasurable difference.

====== Speer said that Hitler was unable to think in either/or terms; he always wanted the one *and* the other.

That was already true in their architectural discussions, and then in the second year of the Russian campaign, with the simultaneous advance on Moscow, Leningrad, Stalingrad and Baku in addition to the arms programmes. He called this Hitler's 'craving for cakes'. He always wanted two pieces on his plate, and if possible a third as well. So, no priorities ever took shape. This should be seen as one of the main reasons for the chaotic steering that afflicted the German conduct of the war.

In this connection, Speer said, mention should also be made of the foolish splitting up of the leadership of the Wehrmacht, which came together again only in the person of Hitler. He was the Supreme Commander, but he intervened here and there at his own discretion; the effects of this were all the more disastrous in that the respective competences of the OKW (Wehrmacht High Command) and the OKH (Army High Command) were never unambiguously defined. In practice the OKH was responsible only for the theatre of operations in the East, so that the chief of the general staff was denied any influence in the other theatres. At the same time, the chiefs of the other two parts of the Wehrmacht had no say in the general conduct of the war and often enough did not even know how the armed forces were distributed.

The consequence of this and many other arbitrary aspects was poor coordination and soon even chaos, especially as the Luftwaffe and the navy operated with a degree of autonomy. In addition there was the conflict between the Wehrmacht and the Party (gauleiters as Reich Defence Commissars). Everyone saw that and tried to influence Hitler as well, but the tangled web of responsibilities corresponded to his favoured chaos principle, which ensured that he always had the last word.

Hitler's suspiciousness, especially with regard to the generals, was another factor standing in the way of a more functional arrangement. Keitel was at least the right man to push through changes, but perhaps he did not even see the need for a department standing directly under the Führer or even for better organization at all. 'In the end he was just a chief clerk for Hitler and had that reputation in the Wehrmacht too.'

───── About the original formulation: Speer described SS Brigadier Hans Kammler (who was responsible for important arms matters in the SS and pestered him a great deal) as a 'Nordic evil angel from Himmler's fiendish stable'. Kammler made a 'stony' impression.

Unfortunately we have not yet managed to get hold of a photo of Kammler. Nor is anything known about his whereabouts. Speer said that all trace of him was lost in the confusion at the end of the war; he seems to have vanished into thin air, 'like a spirit' – which would suit him. Question: why doesn't Speer include a sketch of Kammler in the book? He will give it some thought.

───── Speer said that he interceded for generals Fromm, Zeitzler and Speidel following the coup attempt of 20 July not only because he felt humanly attached to them as a result of long years of common activity. Even more, he wanted to send a signal to Hitler that their friendship had suffered and that he could no longer count on him as a matter of course. This was also not the least of the reasons why he assisted the surviving dependants of the conspirators. We got nowhere asking him for details, as Speer refused to give any information on the grounds that he did not want to 'put on airs'. It was hardly a moral motive that led him to do it, but rather – in addition to the 'little lesson' for Hitler – 'sheer recklessness', probably due to the indifference that was then beginning to come over him.

Nevertheless, Speer added, he was glad that his appointment with Fromm and Stauffenberg at midday on 20 July had not taken place. Even today he cannot say what answer he would have given them. It is fairly certain that he would have rejected their invitation to take part.

===== In answer to a question of ours, Speer said that in the late summer of 1944, shortly after Goebbels had been appointed 'sub-dictator', he again tried to form an alliance with him. They had worked together on the 'total war', he said, and now they should both try to alleviate the pointless hardship for the population (evacuation, etc.). At the time he thought that his chances of winning Goebbels's support for his plan were all the greater because he had repeatedly shown understanding during their discussions and at least not contradicted the criticism of Hitler. But Goebbels simply did not hear what he said. 'Actually he was not a cowardly person', Speer remarked. 'But nor did he have the courage of his convictions.' So Goebbels, who was known in the inner circle as the 'total warrior' or 'Dr Dictator', drew closer to Hitler, while Speer found himself increasingly on the margins.

===== Heidelberg, March 1969. On being asked about his plan to hand himself over to the Allies, which began to pre-occupy him as defeat loomed up, Speer said that it had been a 'crazy idea', romantic and perhaps even childish. He had produced worried faces even among people who thought highly of him, such as generals Thomale and Lüschen. So he soon dropped it.

===== To another question about what motivated him to defy the 'scorched earth' policy, Speer uttered something about duty and responsibility and his view that it was impermissible

to 'chase' into destruction people who had fought so hero-
ically. But somewhere among the many words, which he awkwardly stuttered out as on every emotionally charged occasion,
there appeared a sentence that might be a kind of key. After
the ever more absurd activity for the arms effort, he said, this
new decision gave him something he had always wanted and
probably needed for life itself: a purpose. And, in view of the
situation in which the country found itself, it was the only
meaningful purpose anywhere. 'Can you understand that?'

He added that this probably also had to do with the fact
that he felt no fear during this whole period, unlike all those
powers in the Party who, having constantly spoken of con-
quering the world for the sake of Germany, displayed only
fear and cowardice when the future of Germany was really
on the line. He mentioned General Guderian as one of the
few noteworthy exceptions within the leadership.[2] After a
discussion in which they touched upon Speer's acts of defiance, the general advised him 'just not to lose his head', in
both senses of the term.

He does not want to claim that he was braver than he
really was. But, once he had recognized it as his duty to ward
off self-destruction, everything else was, as always, pushed to
one side, including concern for his family and his own
person. Today he is often blamed for his ruthlessness, but in
this case it was correct and actually necessary, even if he did
not draw out its final consequences.

===== Over the next few days, several discussions with
Siedler about what Speer had said. The key issue for us was
whether anything in his life had ever been more important
than career, success and, if possible, fame. A regulative idea,
one might say. He spoke so awkwardly about 'duty' and
'responsibility' that we were inclined to believe him. But that
only applied from 1943 or 1944 on. Until then he operated

with only himself in mind. And there are still question marks. For him first of all, then for any future biographer. Strange that he has not found one yet.

══════ Speer cannot get away from the idea that Hitler's 'scorched earth' policy was a break with everything he had previously represented. The Hitler quotations that I showed him from the early years (*Mein Kampf*, the speeches, the *Second Book*, etc.) got us nowhere. He spoke of a 'degeneration' in Hitler's thought. Remarkable blindness, even today, but now *post hoc* and from the outside. He sometimes wonders – Speer added after a brief pause – whether Hitler's changes were not due to Morell and the medication that he constantly administered. Towards the end Hitler was truly drug-dependent. I objected that Hitler needed drugs all his life and that, whereas in the early years ideas had served the purpose, he later expanded his consumption to medical drugs.

══════ I asked Speer whether he would have refused orders connected with the 'scorched earth' policy if things had not already reached breaking point with Hitler. I could not get the thought out of my mind that, after so many years of unconditional obedience, he had not found his surprising rebelliousness because of a sense of responsibility for the whole. Rather, his intention had been to pay Hitler back for the way in which he had neglected him during the weeks of illness.

Speer looked bewildered and at first had no answer. Finally he said that everyone needs some stimulus for their behaviour.

══════ Later in the conversation, a remarkable statement by Speer. He sometimes wonders whether – despite all the justifications at the time, which are still valid today – his acts of defiance against the 'scorched earth' policy should not ultimately, at least in a formal sense, be regarded as a 'betrayal'. Likewise his manner at Nuremberg? And now these 'memoirs'. Will the accusation of 'disloyalty' drown out every other aspect when the book is published?

We tried to talk him out of it, but he came back to the subject twice more. Once he added by way of explanation that the reproach would certainly not knock him sideways. He just wants to know whether he should be prepared for it.

===== During the last two or three months before the end, Speer said, he observed on a number of occasions how Goebbels and Ley withdrew with some papers to one of the rooms in the bunker. They looked very important and mysterious, as if they had been entrusted with something out of the ordinary. One could sometimes hear Funk and Bormann going with them. They answered any inquisitive allusions with the inscrutable laughter of the privileged, which evidently was also meant to convey to Speer that he was not one of them. The 'ridiculous cock-fighting of the last phase'.

Only in retrospect, years later, did it occur to him what Goebbels and especially Ley had been up to. He is convinced that, at those meetings, the text was drawn up for what was later published as the famous *Testament politique de Hitler*. Of course, he cannot vouch for this and does not even know whether Hitler checked and approved this last major account of his aims and his regime as well as of the reasons for his failure. But he does think it likely, since neither Goebbels nor Ley would ever have dared to compose such extensive revelations in the first person without showing the text to Hitler.

===== The most unpleasant conversation he ever had with Hitler was on the night of 28 March 1945. In fact, he had

*A photograph of Hamburg in April 1945. In the late stages of the
Second World War, many German towns were destroyed in a hail
of bombs.*

taken a lot of liberties with a memorandum that Hitler had
sent him just before, and he could imagine how angrily this
had been received. As always, he found that he had to face
Hitler openly, and so, to the horror of his own people, he
went over to the Reich Chancellery. Again he noticed the
cold looks everywhere, and as he drew closer everyone hurried off in different directions, as if he had been afflicted
with a kind of leprosy. An orderly appeared and asked him to
follow her. As they walked down the narrow spiral staircase
into the bunker system, he involuntarily thought that the
many steps symbolized something like the downhill road on
which he had been moving for some time.

As soon as he entered the little store-room, he could see
that Hitler felt deeply wounded, and for a moment he experienced something like satisfaction that at least this once he

had pierced the armour with which Hitler surrounded himself. But, of course, that was rather an absurd idea, which did not fit the situation at all.

Hitler was waiting for him just behind the door, and what he first noticed were the veins on his temples. They were all the stranger because he spoke very softly when he began to pour out the reproaches. But, feeling himself to be in the right, Speer, unlike Hitler, remained completely cool and felt the superior person throughout the altercation. He also let Hitler perceive this, by keeping a calm and fixed gaze whatever he said, and he could tell that this ruffled him even more. His continued silence, which probably gave the impression of arrogance, must also have worried Hitler. Of course, Hitler could have ordered him to be killed, and once or twice he imagined how Hitler might walk to the door, shout something down the corridor and have him taken away. Then again he wondered whether he would dare do it. Greater than any fear, however, was his feeling of superiority. Today all this sounds a bit too fantastic. 'But that's how it was.' And a little later: 'I don't enjoy talking about it.'

It was this remarkably fatalistic mood which allowed him to resist Hitler's reproaches so calmly that the latter temporarily lost control of himself. But at some point Hitler suddenly changed his tone and became concerned, almost fatherly. He suggested that he had ended his convalescent leave in Merano too soon and spoke of another holiday that he would like to arrange for him, and so on in the same vein. Hitler's art of persuasion had never before failed to have the intended effect on him, and perhaps the real shock that day for Hitler was that for the first time he gained 'no power over me'. While he was talking, Speer simply thought all the time about the destruction, the desperate people he had met, the streams of refugees and evacuees, who if Hitler had his way were doomed to the utmost misery. That made him so immovable. For, of course, it was clear that what Hitler really wanted was a free hand for his 'scorched earth'. That same day he had given Guderian the push: 'Now I too would be on my way.'

When I asked him to forget everything he had already written about it and to continue in as much detail as possible, he said the following. Until then they had been standing opposite each other in the tiny room, and he could again smell the bad breath coming from Hitler's mouth. Several times Hitler required him to declare his belief in final victory. When they made no headway, Hitler, as if suddenly, became tired, shuffled backwards into the room and sat down at the table. Never had Speer seen him look so frail. His arm was trembling more than ever, and in the awkward stillness he bitterly remarked: 'Amid all the betrayals around me, only misfortune has remained constant; misfortune and my shepherd dog Blondi.' Then he cast a reproachful and resigned look at Speer. 'I understood what he meant.'

The sequel, Speer added, and the way Hitler finally gave him a twenty-four-hour ultimatum are described in the manuscript. There is no more to say than what he has already written. When he went back to the ministry, his liaison officer von Poser, Frau Kempf and the others greeted him as if he had returned from the dead. Then he withdrew and spent hours racking his brains over the one sentence that Hitler wanted – the answer that was not there. He could find no way of finishing it and in the end simply wrote away. Finally he handed the letter to an orderly, and then a call immediately came through demanding that he appear in person at the bunker. 'In the end', Speer concluded, 'when I offered Hitler an empty formula expressing my loyalty instead of the required declarations of confidence, the dispute was settled. I had won!' As he left, the thought occurred to him that Hitler had now laid down his arms, at least in relation to him. But immediately afterwards he dismissed the idea: 'Hitler doesn't capitulate to a subordinate.'

I asked Speer why in the manuscript he did not describe the scene as graphically as he had just now, and why he left unmentioned a number of interesting details. He looked blank for a moment, then said: 'I don't want to!' No attempt to make him change his mind.

⸻ At the last concert of the Berlin Philharmonic, Speer said, he arranged with Gerhart von Westermann (the orchestra manager) and Gerhard Taschner (the leader) that Bruckner's Romantic Symphony would be used as a disaster signal. If the Bruckner symphony was announced, it would be a sign that every musician should escape by the next day at the latest.

Speer also said that virtually none of the musicians heeded the warning; nearly all remained in Berlin. Then he reported a story that had been repeated several times: namely, that after the concert members of the Hitler Youth distributed potassium cyanide capsules at the exit. But he cannot and will not vouch for this; he often thinks it was just one of the numerous rumours doing the rounds in Berlin at that time. All the same, he first heard it when he returned to Pariser Platz after the concert. He then immediately remembered the Hitler Youth members who, unusually, had been walking around near the exits.

I asked him whether he thought the story could have been true. 'But of course!' he said emphatically. 'Absolutely! It was even likely.' Only he had no proof and had therefore refrained from including the episode in the manuscript. Incidentally, around the same time he and some colleagues secured a private concert by his friend Wilhelm Kempff. The whole repertoire of Romantic music. Kempff played for nearly four hours. Unforgettable, considering the situation in which they found themselves, were Chopin's sonata with the funeral march and Beethoven's 'Pathétique'. 'Everyone had tears in their eyes', he ended.

━━━━━ Schloss Korb, near Merano. When I arrived at the breakfast table, Frau Speer was already waiting. I said she would soon be able to breathe more easily, as the book that had obviously caused her so many worries was nearly finished; not much longer and she would be rid of us.

Instead of dismissing the casual remark without much fuss, she became unusually serious and said approximately word for word: 'You must understand! I haven't had many good years. And now I'm afraid all the time that what's left might also go to pieces. I'm not talking about the fact that I never have my husband to myself for a whole day. I'm used to that. But I still have a few memories, and my worry is that they too will be taken from me.' She looked towards the terrace door at which Speer had just appeared. 'You see, he never gives a moment's thought to the fact that we were happy in those days.'

━━━━━ In a retrospective review, Speer again spoke of the figures he had found actually 'insufferable', not just towards whom he had felt indifferent (as he had to most). First he mentioned the crude, in every sense common and 'boozy' (!) Bormann, then his head of the technical bureau, Karl Otto Saur, the 'scheming' Dorsch, the SS doctor and friend of Himmler's Dr Gebhardt, and – after a few appraisals of some second-rank people – surprisingly Ribbentrop. The foreign minister was both 'dull-witted and puffed up', a 'vain nincompoop' who always behaved petulantly in accordance with protocol. Perhaps, Speer said, it had something to do with his sense that everyone around felt complete contempt for him. It was 'impossible to bear him' – the 'stupid' arriviste type. Hitler too soon perceived this and, however much he bowed and scraped, scarcely ever received him during the war.

In the final weeks of the war Speer often saw the foreign minister sitting 'like a dog' at the door of Hitler's rooms, the last time on the night of 23 April during his visit to the Reich Chancellery. He cannot say whether Hitler ever let Ribbentrop in again. Everyone at the Führer's headquarters preferred, as he did, to stick with Walter Hewel, a more obliging and sociable man, who at times gave the impression of being somewhat reckless. Hitler called him in more and more instead of the foreign minister, and perhaps it is too little known that he also liked him personally more than almost anyone else. Speer still finds it incomprehensible that, after the successful break-out from the Reich Chancellery on 2 May, Hewel committed suicide in the cellar of a brewery in Wedding as the Russians were closing in. It was not a fitting end for him.

———— As a kind of addendum, Speer said today that his list of the repulsive people in Hitler's entourage had inadvertently left out one name: Hermann Fegelein. As Himmler's special protégé, Fegelein managed to gain access to Obersalzberg and, as it were, to establish himself there. He was noisy, unscrupulous and a cynical schemer, who boasted more or less openly about his 'roguery'. It was said that, as the head of an SS brigade on the Eastern front, he acquired the reputation of being the leader of a 'gang of homicidal arsonists'. In Spandau, Funk told him of the saying that 'where Fegelein goes, there are no more villages, no more people, no more life.'

It fits the picture, Speer added, that Fegelein was quick-witted and a good entertainer. At the Berghof he quite shamelessly paid 'court' to lonely women. He was even noticed on various occasions trailing after Eva Braun. As the spoiled women's heart-throb that he took himself to be (and probably also was), he was not at all embarrassed to carry on in the way that he did. It is well known that in summer 1944 he married Eva Braun's sister, Gretl. But Speer never got the suspicion out of his mind that Fegelein basically had his eye on the more attractive Eva; many rumours circulating in the Berghof even claimed that she had wanted to win him, had been the instigating party, and had wanted to make provisions for the time after Hitler. Speer himself never observed that. In any event, Fegelein did not give up his advances even after his marriage to Gretl Braun. He was a thoroughly depraved character, 'one of the most disgusting people I've ever come across'.

A little later, Speer added that Fegelein's execution, ordered by Hitler on one of the last days of April, has always seemed to him a just end. According to Fritzsche in Nuremberg, when the head of the Wachtruppe, SS Brigade Leader Hans Rattenhuber, or his henchmen were taking Fegelein to be executed, he kept screaming and directed the coarsest abuse at the SS unit. Evidently he had been unable to imagine that his run of good luck would one day come to an end. Fritzsche too only knew such details from hearsay. Easy to believe, though, Speer said. For Fegelein always had a tendency to effrontery, having succeeded with it all his life.

══════ I said I thought it was regrettable that, on the whole, his family scarcely features in these memoirs, and I asked Speer whether he would not like to insert a passage or two about it. But he replied: 'My family doesn't appear in this book because it hasn't appeared in my life.' He has neglected the family more than even a workaholic is permitted to do; this often weighs on his mind. He referred to the failure of the family reunion after his release from detention. Everyone made the most earnest of efforts and for that very reason contributed to the 'nightmare' that remained in everyone's memory. He too. Then he suddenly broke off, as if he had already gone too far by dropping these hints.

6

COMPLETION OF THE *MEMOIRS*

May 1969, the Waltershof in Kampen. Last meeting to complete the work. At first Siedler and I alone, and Siedler exasperated that in the already passed final draft of the manuscript Speer has again inserted five or six confessions of guilt which, though sincerely meant, are rather stereotyped in terms of content – in addition, that is, to the three or four that the manuscript anyway contains. 'That won't bring any of the dead back to life', Siedler said excitedly. 'He still hasn't grasped that the whole effort has to go into making processes vivid: the mechanisms of denial, self-mollification, moral deafness, compliance, and so on. Instead he always wants to say how sorry he is for everything.' But when Speer joined us in the early afternoon, Siedler had calmed down and said that he was willing to print the manuscript as it is.

I did not agree and disturbed the splendid harmony. Right at the beginning of our walk from the Waltershof to the Watt, I mentioned to Speer that he would have to delete the new additions. Objectively I had an easy time of it, as

I simply had to repeat the points Siedler had made in the morning. Siedler wriggled with embarrassment, and of course it was clear to me that I was showing him up before Speer. But the two of us were so united, and he had been so indignant, that I felt obliged to go ahead with this little exposure. Later I apologized to him and said that we had been manoeuvring long enough with Speer's empty scenes of remorse; now we finally had to stand by our convictions. Speer was openly disgruntled, especially with me, but he accepted the cuts. Back in the hotel, I got down to the deletions before his very eyes. He looked depressed.

===== This morning we asked Speer whether he had forgotten, obscured or concealed any important event, especially anything that might be incriminating; it would certainly be better for his reputation and his credibility if he took the initiative in speaking about it, instead of later having to justify himself if, for example, an angry or ill-willed former colleague made some accusations against him. That would put him in a hopeless situation and might have irreparable consequences.

Speer said he had been prepared for this question and that in the previous weeks he had checked through everything. He had examined with an especially critical eye all the crucial points that might offer 'a handle for someone with bad intentions'. But he could say with a clear conscience that there was nothing like that; there were 'no secrets'.

Before we parted, Speer gave me as a token of his gratitude a watercolour that Hitler painted in his Vienna years. It shows the Minorite Church in Vienna, in the postcard style. Hitler gave it to Speer in 1939 for his numerous personal services. Speer said it might be useful for my book. And indeed a large part of Hitler's character is expressed in the picture, not only in relation to the Vienna period: his

Speer speaking at the Berlin Sportspalast, June 1943

dependence on guidelines, his reverence for the past, his aloofness from people, his pedantry. Also his petty-bourgeois taste in art, which only later, under the influence of Hans Posse,[1] broke through to somewhat broader horizons. Speer said that I should find it stimulating. He has clearly got over the tensions of the last few days and wants to supply me with another statement of authenticity.

===== Siedler has sent me the first copy of the *Memoirs*, enclosing a brief handwritten letter. He speaks of 'many clouds' that have accompanied our work on the book, and calls them the 'result of disturbing experiences' that we either got the author to talk about or had to wrest from him.

===== A call from Speer about this and that. He shows an unaffected pleasure in the success of the book and asks the publishing house almost every day for the latest sales figures.

The old intoxication with figures is reappearing, I threw in. Only this time, he replied, the story behind it is absolutely innocuous.

===== Frankfurt Book Fair. Siedler tells of an experience with Jerry Gross, the manager of the American Macmillan publishing company, which is bringing out the *Memoirs*. After discussing it with him earlier, Speer invited Gross to join him for a meal and then, on a sudden impulse, asked whether he would not like to bring his wife too. Gross hesitated at first, but as he found Speer honest and likeable he eventually agreed. But his wife refused the invitation point blank. She supposedly said that she would never sit at the same table anywhere with a Nazi like Speer. Surprisingly, however, Speer then got put through to her and finally persuaded her to change her mind.

Siedler reported that during the meal, where the forms were friendly if a little forced, Mrs Gross scarcely said a word. But when she returned with her husband to their apartment and closed the door behind them, she took a few, suddenly uncertain steps, sank into a nearby chair and began to weep in spasms. She wept and wept, and was almost inconsolable. Hours passed before she regained her composure.

===== Speer reported the rising tide of gossip behind his back; new indications have been reaching him nearly every day. Sometimes he wonders whether he did not go too far in condemning the regime and Hitler, as this may have damaged the pedagogical effect he intended the book to have. He is also pained by the loss of many friends and former close colleagues. He is constantly being told the names of new people who have distanced themselves from him. He hopes that time will straighten out some of these things. In any event, these difficulties have been worrying him more than he thought they would. But he does not doubt that what he has done is right. After the conversation it seemed to me that he does doubt it, and far more than he lets on.

═════ Speer reported that Golo Mann, in his review of the *Memoirs*, wrote that he (Speer) had twice jumped ahead in his career because of someone's death (Troost and Todt); that too was part of the pact with the devil. He feels understood by Golo Mann better than by anyone else. He laid special emphasis on the Chamisso ballad with which the review ends ('Die Männer im Zoptenberge'); he has made a note of the key lines, which tell of how the men lower their eyes when asked if they feel sorry for their disgraceful deeds. They 'took fright and were speechless', the ballad continues. 'They did not know it themselves.' It's as if it was written with him in mind.

Speer said that, of course, it did happen that he gained office through someone else's death. He saw a 'demonic force' at work in this, although it never even remotely occurred to him to draw any conclusion from it. The spirit of the demonic elevated all of them in those days and, so to speak, brought home to them the greatness of the hour and their own vocation. How could they have had any second thoughts?

═════ On the publication of the French edition of the *Memoirs* in Paris. In the evening, invited by the publisher to a restaurant near the Pont St Michel. Among the guests was Jean d'Ormesson, who (obviously thinking not least of figures like Speer) called Germany an 'eternal *terra incognita*', a peculiar combination of 'ambitious plans and bizarre, outlandish petty-bourgeois attitudes'. Also François-Poncet, who had a nodding acquaintance with Speer when he was French ambassador in Berlin in the 1930s.

Before we sat down to eat, François-Poncet said that many of those he had told of his acceptance of the invitation were astonished and did not suppress a frown. He had replied that they should not put on airs: far too many French people were in the grip of the victor's arrogance. Besides, most of them had only just 'got away with it', and he wished that they were more aware of this. He had known Hitler and his 'phoney genius'. So he knew a thing or two about the problem in which Speer had been caught up.

===== January 1971, Speer and Siedler in Frankfurt. Now that the book has been published and brought psychological closure, Speer is evidently thinking of a second career as an architect. In any case, he took us to the office of an architect he has befriended and showed us some expertly detailed sketches for a functional building, a packing shed with a large office section. He was also involved in planning a brewery complex. A lengthy discussion. Both Siedler and I advised against it. You cannot design 'Germania' and then a beer factory somewhere in Schleswig-Holstein. But, as Speer said, he needs to have a task again.

Later in the evening, at a pub outside town, thoughts on what should happen to the piles of notebooks/secret messages that Speer smuggled out of Spandau prison. The Federal Archives. Siedler asked whether a book could be made out of them; everything he has seen of them suggests that this is a real possibility. Speer seemed almost happy that the question had been raised, and in particular that Siedler trusted him to handle it.

===== Next morning, a trip to the Führer's 'Eyrie' headquarters not far from Bad Nauheim. The complex, a manor house

The only known visit by Speer to a concentration camp: Mauthausen, early 1943. To the left of Speer is the Upper Danube gauleiter August Eingruber.

with outbuildings, is well concealed and partly built into the hillside. Speer recently calculated that, by the end of the war, Hitler had a dozen or more headquarters, many of which he used either never or only for a few days, as well as many that were never finished. The most costly was the 'Wolf's Gorge' near Margival, but Hitler occupied that headquarters for only six to eight hours. The Berghof and the 'Führer's special train' should also be added to the reckoning, the latter having served both for journeys and as a headquarters.

Basing himself only on photographs and building plans, Hitler rejected as 'too lavish' the first headquarters that Speer built for him before the offensive of May–June 1940 in the West. He refused to spend a single day there: it was not his style, he indignantly remarked, but rather a conception for a 'noble horse breeder'.

But over the years, Speer said later, the various headquarters became more and more gigantic. Once he tried to calculate the number of construction workers (still nearly 30,000 at the end of the war) and the quantities of cable and concrete that this required; dozens of new roads and bridges also had to be built for the access routes. On one occasion, he remarked to Poser that it looked as if Hitler was striving to achieve the dimensions of the new Berlin in his own headquarters, as a substitute for the work that was not making headway in the capital itself. One of the last headquarters on which work began was not far from Breslau, but it was overrun by the Red Army before it could be completed. It bore the cover name 'Giant'. 'In a kind of parallel with the monster tank known by the diminutive "Mousey", we jokingly talked about it as the "Führer Headquarters Dwarf".'

====== Speer thoroughly taken with the new edition. Suddenly wants to rush back to his desk in Heidelberg. Already has suggestions for the title: either 'The Third Twenty Years' or 'My Third Life'. He would like to place as a motto at the front of the book: 'A la recherche du temps perdu'. I strongly advise against. That shoe does not suit him and is also a few sizes too big. Speer looks irritated. True, his book of memoirs is a considerable success, with around 100,000 copies. But does he therefore think he is a major writer? He has told some significant stories for our understanding of the period. But that does not mean he has become important in literary terms.

====== With Speer and the erstwhile Field-Marshal Milch at the 'Breidenbacher Hof'. Nicolaus von Below, Hitler's air force adjutant, the historian David Irving and Johannes Gross also there.[2] Earlier, Speer had some worries that Milch, who before a meal sometimes got into an expansive

'wine mood', would propose a toast and – as Speer had often
seen – say something in appreciation of Hitler, 'not uncritical, of course, but a little ranting' and anyway not appropriate for the semi-public venue of an elegant Düsseldorf
restaurant.

To avoid any problems, Siedler gave a little speech himself
as soon as we were seated in the far corner of the restaurant
that Speer had reserved for us. He spoke of the inevitably
varying images of history that everyone who lived through
such times has preserved, and did not forget to mention his
own prison sentence, which naturally made him think back
to those years in a different way from people who had occupied leadership positions. He formulated the final words in
such a conclusive manner that it was impossible for anyone
to give a counter-speech, and Milch, who had evidently seen
through Siedler's ploy, laughed contentedly: 'No, no! I'm not
planning to make a speech.' He talked about the tensions
with Speer and the fact that they had nevertheless become
friends. In the last months of the war, he said, Speer had
behaved 'in a completely crazy way', but they had all been
crazy then; neither he nor any of his trustworthy friends had
been able to understand 'what was driving Speer'. But 'he
impressed us all a great deal'.

Later, an argument between Irving and myself. Irving
claimed something like exclusive rights to an episode related
by von Below (Hitler's farewell to the Berghof in mid-July
1944); I was not supposed to use it in my forthcoming biography of Hitler. He was loud and boorish, and then he repeated
his well-known thesis. He insisted that he was the only historian of the Hitler period who worked on the basis of the
sources; all the rest were just 'copiers'. Speer tried to mediate,
but did not get far until Milch called over to Irving in a
peremptory tone: 'That's enough now!' Irving immediately
fell silent and started to fiddle with the food on his plate.

▬▬▬ With Hugh Trevor-Roper. We soon came to Speer, and he told of his discussions with him immediately after the war in Schleswig-Holstein and in September in Kransberg. Speer had impressed him with his candour, insight and precise memory. He was not at all obdurate or self-opinionated, unlike all the others with whom he, Trevor-Roper, had spoken. Nor without dignity. The others were complete 'clowns', the 'latrine-cleaner' or 'buffoon' type (all this in a very idiomatic German!). But Speer stood out from them, and Trevor-Roper was also impressed by the calmness with which he awaited his fate. He found in him a figure he had not thought possible and – the more he thinks about it – one who cannot actually exist: the cultivated Nazi.

Trevor-Roper has not yet read the *Memoirs*, but he said he will get down to them in the next few days. He wanted to hear my opinion of Speer, and I told him of our work, of Speer's constant mistrust for a while, but also of the reservations on my side. We largely agreed about the contradictions and puzzles that Speer posed. Trevor-Roper said he wonders whether the confessions of guilt that one hears from Speer are not also just the expression of a by now habitual contradictoriness, as if he wants to keep a more visible distance than before from people he has always held in contempt. Then about the *Spandau Diaries*, on which work is currently being done.

At the end Trevor-Roper said he has been toying with the idea of writing a biography of Speer, or perhaps a long biographical essay like the one on Philby. For Speer, precisely because of his contradictions, is the key figure for what happened in 1933 and the following period. The Streichers or Sauckels pose no questions. The 'social criminal' or 'political desperado' types, as he called them, can be found in every society, including in Britain. It does not take long to get on top of them.

The puzzling thing about Germany, Trevor-Roper continued, is its orderly citizens, who at that time went over in droves to the Nazis. That did not happen anywhere else, and so Speer was something like a representative of those who went over. What happened? What failed everyone? Education, parental home, university? Moral standards? He cannot help thinking that a biography of Speer might throw more light on what historians have grappled with for years but have made no great progress in explaining.

I vigorously encouraged him. Trevor-Roper asked about materials and persons. Among others I mentioned Wolters, Hettlage, Rohland, Milch, von Below and von Poser. I also offered to get hold of the addresses for him. As we parted, I had the impression that he wanted to get down to the project in the near future.

===== Thinking over what Trevor-Roper said. At a personal level, the pictures largely tally with each other. No doubt Speer is likeable, intelligent and insightful in discussion. But I ask myself whether it is not precisely the civilized features that make him and his ilk so alarming. For, if even a man with his education, his standards and his thoroughly moral sensitivity to the crime around him not only found nothing offensive but was able to sit at the same table with the criminals, then where was the line drawn? Evidently there is none. It is all quite fathomless. Paradoxically it is not the Streichers or Sauckels or Trevor-Roper's 'political criminals' who are so disturbing; their like do indeed exist in every society. To some extent, you can read from their face what is to be expected from them. From Speer's, on the other hand, you can read nothing, or only the wrong things. They bring a whole picture of man crashing down.

The measures preparing for major road construction in Berlin included the clearance of tens of thousands of homes, many of them owned by Jews. Speer's department took on this job, as is clear from this note which became public only after Speer's death.

Maybe the problem lies precisely in the immeasurable difference between a cultivated appearance and the baneful political role that Speer played.

A call from Speer about an article that the Harvard lecturer Erich Goldhagen has published about him in an American journal. Goldhagen tries to demonstrate, in opposition to the account in the *Memoirs*, that Speer was present for the speech in Poznań in which Himmler made his appalling revelations about the mass murder of the Jews. A momentary suspicion that there are 'secrets' after all which Speer, despite his assurances, concealed in our discussions.

Speer complained that Goldhagen was either mistaken or prejudiced against him. He is absolutely certain that he left Poznań before Himmler's speech. He sounded very upset, but also insecure, and the whole South German calmness that sometimes makes you think he is talking of something rather alien that only marginally affects him was suddenly gone. He kept saying that the article left him 'stunned': the word came up six or eight times. At any rate, his agitation made it clear to me that the 'cardinal question' of his life was at issue.

When his agitation had subsided a little, Speer said that he has quite a reliable memory; no one knows that better than I. But since reading Goldhagen's attacks he has suddenly become suspicious: 'I can no longer believe myself.' He wants to produce evidence that he was not present for Himmler's truly appalling speech – which he first heard about only a considerable time later – but he does not yet know how. He must do it, so that he can 'trust himself again'.

Three days later. Another call from Speer. He is hardly one step further. But he has regained his impassive tone and speaks in a friendly Heidelberg sing-song about the research he is doing. A sense of having heard him once insecure and without a ready answer. But it's already over. An enigmatic person. Afterwards a telephone conversation with Siedler. He too has received several confused calls from Speer in the past days. He said he could not fully understand his agitated state, but I replied that such a clear-thinking mind must be muddled by the question of whether it can still believe itself (as Speer put it to me). For that is clearly the main reason for his concern. Just imagine, I said, how everything can break down if the reliability of your memory is impaired.

Siedler agreed on the whole, but he said that even worse for Speer was the worry that he might be caught out telling a lie – 'if there was one'. I disagreed. What does one lie matter after a life in a camorra? I said. In general, I attach no special moral weight to Goldhagen's accusation. For any observer who knows himself free of Goldhagen's petty career interests, the question of whether Speer attended Himmler's notorious speech in Poznań is of no importance. Or, anyway, of third-rate importance. Speer knew enough, in detail, about the crimes of the regime to be guilty. After a couple of objections, Siedler concurred.

Then once more about Speer's unfocused way of being in the world and relating to it. Sometimes, I said, he gives the impression that he is still a prisoner to noble-sounding formulas and is simply unable to dispense with them. Siedler said he has quite often had the feeling with Speer that, on the critical issues, one is biting on plastic. Recently he asked himself how often we had managed to break through that attitude.

'A funny idea!' I said. And he: 'No, not funny. More a cause for alarm.'

======= Again a few days later. Speer said that his former colleague Walter Rohland, whom he had come across by chance and told of the Goldhagen article and his own deep dismay, had calmed him down for the time being. They had left Poznań together around midday; Speer had been at the wheel of his personal Mercedes and driven it 'like a racing driver' along the sometimes bumpy roads; they had reached the Führer's headquarters at Rastenberg in the evening. Not the least of the reasons why he could be so sure of all this was that he had checked the facts for his own recently composed memoirs.

======= (*Addendum*: Gitta Sereny, in her book *Das Ringen mit der Wahrheit. Albert Speer und das deutsche Trauma*,[3] repeats the damaging claim of Harvard professor Erich Goldhagen that Speer, contrary to his stubbornly maintained testimony, did attend Heinrich Himmler's speech in

Poznań on 6 October 1943. The speech is so notorious because the SS Führer spoke there with brutal frankness about the extermination of the Jews. Speer insists that he left the conference around midday and cites two witnesses: Walter Rohland, head of the 'Ruhr Staff', who made a name for himself mainly in the field of tank production; and Dr Harry Siegmund, who was in charge of organizing the Poznań event. Both men have testified in an affidavit that Speer left Poznań some time before the speech that Himmler gave in the late afternoon.

Against this, Gitta Sereny claims that Speer extracted the statements from the two witnesses, and that the 'most likely explanation' for Walter Rohland's support is that he was 'a good friend of Speer's'. As to Harry Siegmund: who knows 'how many calls Speer bombarded him with' until he finally handed over the statement demanded of him?

In autumn 1999, after a reading and discussion of my recently published biography of Speer in a Kiel bookshop, one of the people present introduced himself to me as Harry Siegmund. He had little trouble addressing the subject of Gitta Sereny's assertion that Speer had 'bombarded' him with requests to confirm his departure from Poznań before Himmler's speech.

There is not a word of truth in it, Siegmund said. In fact, already in late 1975, after a report in *Der Spiegel* about Goldhagen's accusations, he let Speer know that he would happily make himself available if he ever needed a witness. In any event, he was willing to confirm in writing the untruthfulness of Goldhagen's claim.

Thereupon Speer replied to him, but they 'only had one telephone conversation'; there were no long discussions apart from that. For he remembered quite clearly that Speer had left the Poznań conference around midday in the company of Walter Rohland. It is a mystery to him how Frau

Sereny arrived at her claim that Speer continually pestered him with telephone calls. Siegmund has made the same points in his own review of his life. He confirmed the facts in a letter he wrote to me.)

━━━ In Heidelberg with Alexander Mitscherlich, who had asked me to bring Speer along. The evening at Mitscherlich's home: a collector's ornamental cup and saucer, little crocheted mats on the glass top of the coffee table, a professor's interior. Mitscherlich, as always, interested and curious in a likeable way. His thoughtful remarks, if sometimes a little pat, are so uninhibited that one spontaneously wonders whether he sees Speer as the 'repentant sinner' or the 'case' that will advance our knowledge. It emerged from some of his questions that, like us, he found Speer's ostensible ignorance scarcely credible.

His other main concern was to find out how Speer had coped with the twenty years of imprisonment, whether he had developed 'self-preservation techniques' and, if so, whether they had helped him. Speer spoke in detail of his 'escapes' into long periods of sleep, his reading programmes, imaginary visits to the theatre, and so on. Later the discussion turned to how he had always found the strength of will to live and avoided sinking into lethargy and existential fatalism. Then about remembrance and the unconscious selection processes that must have shaped his retrospective vision, inevitably resulting in a picture formed in advance. Then for a long while about the Schreber case, which for some time has been the subject of much discussion among psychologists.

Towards the end Mitscherlich asked whether Speer had been able to develop his special relationship with Hitler, and to rise so high, precisely because he had been non-political and therefore, unlike nearly all the other Party people in the

entourage, not a competitor for power. Discussion about the
Nazi Party as a gathering-point for apolitical types.

Throughout the evening it was hard to take Frau M.'s
constant eagerness to add a word of her own, and unfortunately over the hours the number of such words came to a few
hundred. Mitscherlich, who was obviously used to her inter-
ventions, was very indulgent through his silences and
extremely understanding, with a gentle smile accustomed to
everyday capitulation.

===== Speer told of his new close friend Carl Zuckmayer,
with whom he has been corresponding for some time and
exchanging visits. When asked about the content of their discussions, Speer was rather unforthcoming. As one might have
suspected, his statements generally come down to the fact
that Zuckmayer keeps returning to Speer's conflict after the
spring and autumn of 1944: Klessheim, the September letter,
the planned assassination, the actions he took against the
'scorched earth', and the way in which generals, gauleiters or
leading figures in the economy reacted when he asked them
to contravene the policy. Also questions about Udet, Kehrl
and other colleagues of Speer. Zuckmayer once said that he
was understandably interested mainly in 'dilemma situations':
how people coped with them, where the breaking point
came, and which character traits meant that it came quite
early in some people, while others put up with considerable
strain.

Speer said a little later that he always found impressive
Zuckmayer's 'professional understanding' of hopeless situations. In fact, nothing human is alien to him. He approaches
even painful failures with impartiality. This does not mean
that he avoids the reprehensible nature of Hitler's rule – after
all, Zuckmayer eventually emigrated. But he does not thrust
it self-righteously into the foreground, as most people do.

Speer added that he had said this appreciatively to Zuck-mayer just a short time ago, and let him know how rare it was. Zuckmayer replied that moral judgement can only ever come at the end; it is not basically something that should be told to the whole world, but should be sorted out by every-one for themselves. In any event, he despises the judge-like public posture that a growing number of people adopt. Most are just play-acting anyway. In reality, what counts for them is less to make strict standards readily discernible than to certify their own great integrity. It displays nothing other than the old Nazi arrogance, but nowadays it turns up in shabbier garb.

Zuckmayer also said that anyone who wishes to be reason-ably forearmed against 'future Hitlers' would do better to understand people than to judge them. When I wanted to know how Speer had replied, he said that he had not thought it his place to give an affirmative answer. And so he had kept silent. For nor could he have rejected Zuckmayer's state-ment, as it was 'simply true'.

═══ September 1973, Berlin. Reception at Siedler's for the publication of my Hitler biography. Full house, publish-ers, friends and people from everywhere. To the question of what the subject would have said about the book, Speer drops the almost casual remark that Hitler sometimes said he wanted to go down in history as a man 'like there has never been in the world before'. He might have thought that the very scope of the book, as well as the cool seriousness with which it describes his life, showed that this had not been a vain ambition. In his exaggerated way, he would have seen it as confirmation. A long discussion about this.

When I later asked Speer in astonishment whether Hitler himself had used the words 'like there has never been in the world before' to express his claim to uniqueness, or whether it was a formulation he had derived from Hitler's statements and actions, Speer replied: 'Literally, of course!' He remembers hearing it from Hitler, several times even.

Once, in late 1938 or a little later, anyway before the outbreak of war, Hitler even justified the rather presumptuous assertion. His life's goal, he said, had always been to make a name for himself in four ways: as a programmatic thinker who understood more than others about the evils of the world; as a successful statesman; as a patron and even founder of the arts, including architecture; and one day as an invincible military commander. Hitler added by way of clarification that the great men of the past, from Alexander to Frederick and Napoleon, had always excelled in only one or another of these fields – Frederick and Napoleon, the two outstanding exceptions, in two of them. But to no significant figure in history had it been granted to win fame in all four. He was sure that he would be the first to achieve that. He wanted to set a new standard.

Feeling rather taken aback, I asked Speer why he had never mentioned that before. The remark struck me as one of the most important things Hitler had said about himself, more revealing than almost any other; it showed in which gallery of historical figures he had seen himself. I could even imagine that I would have placed it as an epigraph at the beginning of the book.

But Speer attached no special weight to it. 'That's how he always spoke', he said; it was just another proof of the delusions of grandeur that he had at that time. Again I sensed Speer's peculiar failure of judgement, his oddly rudderless thinking for a man of his intelligence. But that is not the least of the things which, in my view, make him representative.

===== (*Addendum*. It should not go unmentioned that this note refers to the reception that a colleague I had just employed for the *Frankfurter Allgemeine Zeitung* has since

By summer 1944 at the latest, the Allies had almost unlimited control of the skies over Germany, and as early as May of that year Speer noted in a memorandum that the outcome of the war was 'decided'. The picture shows victims of a raid on the Berlin Sporthalle in 1944.

elevated to the status of a scandal. Neither I nor the host nor anyone else I have asked noticed that Speer's presence there caused offence to any of the guests. Even the journalist in question, during the following twenty-six years of close collaboration, never dropped so much as a hint about his feelings of outrage, until the publication of his own 'memoirs'. He has said in his defence that he kept silent so as not to jeopardize his chances at the *Frankfurter Allgemeine Zeitung*. But that simply means his behaviour has been as adaptive as that of the Germans in the 1930s whom he has again and again reproached for their opportunism.

In conclusion, it should be said that the supposed scandal is an invention, both in general and in the particulars. I shall therefore not explain it in this text.)

===== One more reaction to the *Memoirs*. Frau Speer assured her children, and on occasion Siedler and myself, that she would never read what her husband had written there. But since everyone has been talking about the book, with no end to the echoes it has produced, it has evidently not been possible for her to keep fending off all the people who ask for her opinion by saying that she is not familiar with the book. Besides, it would appear from a lot of statements that no one believes her, and it may be this and other reasons that have finally led her to read the *Memoirs* after many years have passed, albeit with visible distaste.

Speer reported today that his wife audibly slammed the book shut as she finished reading it, then came across the room and said to him in an uncharacteristically heated tone: 'Life hasn't left me with much. But now you've ruined all that remained!'

ON THE END AND THE FAREWELL TO

HITLER

No notes for nearly a year, although some must have gone missing. Not in close touch with Speer – roughly one call every three months. But nothing worth reporting, apart from scanty remarks concerning the progress of his work on the book about his prison years. Speer speaks of 'great difficulties', the huge mountain of papers that he secretly got out of the cell at Spandau and once poured out in front of us to be arranged. Also a lot of handwritten stuff that even he can scarcely decipher.

At work again for a week. This time Sylt once more. Otherwise the same group, the same technique, the same discussions. We talked about the 'dramaturgical problem' involved in this book, unlike the *Memoirs*. Before, he could allow himself to be led and carried along as the author of the historical events. This time he does not have such a guide rope. The task is to make the reader conscious of the sluggishly passing time, while still making it 'entertaining'; to render the monotony perceptible without becoming monotonous oneself. A lot of suggestions, which Speer carefully noted down and took with him to Heidelberg.

━━━━━ September 1974, Stutenhof. Speer has made a revised version of his thousands of notes from Spandau prison, and on Sylt I read the manuscript. Still much too detailed, plus a lot of repetitions. Speer himself said it was just a draft, nothing more. But he wants to finish the work in April next year. Siedler is expected only tomorrow.

━━━━━ Speer in a talkative mood today. Yesterday, when I had finished the inevitably cursory reading and given Speer some fundamental comments, I took the opportunity to ask him once more about his final visit to the Reich Chancellery, at the end of April 1945. In the *Memoirs*, despite all our remonstrations, he dealt with the incident only in passing. Now too he said that he did not want to insert anything further about the episode into the Spandau notes, but finally, after a brief and possibly suspicious glance, he started up in a rather faltering manner. Gradually he spoke more freely, so that at one point I thought it was almost too free for the most dramatic moment of his life, and certainly the one when he came closest to death. There had always been something about it that I found difficult to understand, especially in view of the unemotional description in the *Memoirs* which suggested he was concealing something, and which he incomprehensibly shortened again in comparison with the original version. Here is an orderly and abbreviated account of what he expressed with a degree of confusion.

His flight on 23 April to an almost totally encircled Berlin was, of course, a lunatic act, and he would probably not have done it for Hitler's sake alone. The imprisonment of Dr Brandt, the lack of a farewell to his friend Friedrich Lüschen (head of the electrical industry) and many other reasons were also required to motivate him to leave – or so he still thinks today. In any event, he is glad that he disregarded the innumerable doubts expressed by nearly everyone, and still feels grateful to his liaison officer, von Poser, for the support he received from him. At Rechlin he was lucky enough to find an aircraft, a fighter no less, because he could have made no headway on the blocked roads.

On his arrival at the Reich Chancellery, as he was crossing the main courtyard, he suddenly thought that he might be shot here in a couple of hours, and then, looking back from the top step, wondered what place the head of the firing squad would choose for the execution. I briefly interrupted to ask whether he was not being too 'melodramatic' about the situation. But he dodged my question by switching to a bald description. The emblematic rooms and galleries were filled with ammunition boxes, sacks of provisions and even a couple of field kitchens. Already in the entrance area he everywhere came across stunned and sometimes almost grateful faces; Hitler's valet Linge immediately broke the first ground. Then he went down the long corridor to the bunker. The heavy masonry was broken in places, and people were wading through large puddles on the plaster floor.

Circumstances had decreed that he should bump into Bormann in the bunker at the foot of the spiral staircase, and he remembers the sense of satisfaction he felt at seeing him almost tremble because of the approaching end. Bormann again put on the false display of affability that had always aroused his disgust. Bormann said he had always known that Speer was one of the Führer's real friends, then said something about 'overwhelming joy' and a 'human and historical gesture' that would 'never be forgotten in the future'. What he really wanted was that Speer should try everything ('No one has as much influence as you on the Führer') to talk Hitler into decamping to Obersalzberg; the best ideas had always come to him there, in the seclusion of his beloved mountain, and he would find the 'knack' (he really said 'knack') of dividing our enemies or a solution that would still allow us to turn things round. The Führer had recently been very resigned, and only an old friend like Speer could drive away his despondency. He (Speer) simply grew angry at Bormann's insincerity and left him standing there.

Everyone with whom he spoke told of the obviously unprecedented scene of frenzy that morning, when the news arrived that the Oder front had also been broken in the north and General Steiner's relief attack had not taken place. All those who had gathered in the corridors and at the door to the map room gave a different account of Hitler's outburst of screaming, which sometimes lapsed into speechlessness and apparently once into sobbing. But everyone still had the terror written over their face, as it were.

After the fit and a short conference with Keitel and a couple of others, Hitler said that under these conditions he was no longer either able or willing to lead, and he retired white as a sheet to his private rooms. One person after another, individually or in a group of two or three, went to speak with him once more: Keitel, Dönitz and General Burgdorf, Goebbels and Fegelein, Bormann and whoever else. They all tried to urge that the situation was by no means hopeless. Hitler, some reported, only listened in silence. But Schaub, Hitler's personal adjutant, said he had been ordered to destroy Hitler's private papers – which was an answer in itself. With the help of the escort, he had many trunks and files taken up into the garden and burned. It was the sign that the end had come. 'Anyway I didn't meet anyone who still had any hope.'

Everyone looked rather shaken, and one of the secretaries warned him: 'Be careful not to get him worked up! The Führer's nerves are terribly on edge.' Speer had a quite eerie feeling, and already on his way from the Brandenburg Gate to the Reich Chancellery he had wondered whether Hitler would receive him with indifference and possibly tears, or whether he would send for a firing squad. Hitler had always been unpredictable and erratic in his decisions, towards the end of the war more so than ever.

When he entered the room, Hitler gave the impression of being very busy and taken up with pressing official business. Bent over his papers, he got Speer to report on his trip to Hamburg, and once even threw in a remark, but when Speer tried to draw him out he became impatient and asked what he thought of Dönitz, who was 'also up there'. In a rather jumbled reply, Speer said something about the grand admiral's strategic sense and reliability, and praised his comradeliness and patriotism. But, while he was speaking, Hitler suddenly pushed his papers aside and asked whether he should remain in Berlin or make his way to Obersalzberg. The argument he had often heard from Goebbels in the past few days then came to mind: that the Führer should await the final outcome in the capital of the Reich, not in his 'summerhouse'. That is what he now advised him to do. Hitler seemed almost relieved and, without any transition, began to speak of his inevitable death.

Then Hitler launched into one of his long and rambling monologues, but with long pauses during which he kept chewing at his nails. In the ever recurring silences, Speer could hear only the noise of the diesel engine that drove the ventilation system, punctuated now and then by the arrival of adjutants or employees, at least a dozen times altogether. Once Bormann entered to report that Ribbentrop was waiting outside and would not go away from the door until the Führer found time for him. This abrupt coming and going was a sign that the neglect of established forms, already observable for some time, had gone even further. When I asked what Hitler actually said, Speer replied that it was 'just the usual stuff'. But surely not, I insisted. In earlier years, the things he always said about architecture, the harm caused by smoking, the breeding of shepherd dogs and so on had been among his favourite subjects.

No, not those things – Speer said, looking visibly strained, as if the discussion was beginning to trouble him. Rather, Hitler spoke of his great objectives and the tremendous things he had intended for the Germans and the world. But no one had understood him; he had found only lack of comprehension even among his oldest comrades, only cowardice, hypocrisy and baseness of character. They had all persuaded themselves that he did not notice! In fact, nothing had remained hidden to him, but he had kept it to himself. After the victory, though, he would have settled accounts – not least with the generals who had deceived and betrayed him. And after another pause: his time would come, he was sure of that.

Curiously, Hitler gave the impression throughout of being remarkably calm and resigned to a fate that was not fitting for him, so that to Speer he cut a more alien figure than ever before. Just a few days previously, on his birthday, for example, Hitler had seemed almost galvanized amid all the stresses and strains. That was now all over, like that morning's emotional outburst. Involuntarily Speer wondered whether Morell, before leaving Berlin, had not given him a tranquillizing injection that was continuing to work.

With an almost tortured sigh, Speer went on to say that Hitler's fury only occasionally broke through, especially when Goering's name came up. Once, towards the end, he drove the pencil he was holding with both hands (because of his trembling) so forcefully into the table top that it broke. Under no circumstances, Hitler said, would he go out to meet the Russians with a weapon in his hand. The danger would be too great of falling into their hands alive. He had also given orders that his body should be immediately cremated, as he feared that it might be 'dishonoured' even in death.

Then someone came into the room again and there was another pause. In all, his visit went on for several hours, with another interruption for a situation conference at which the main topic was whether the ring around the city had already closed and how much longer it would be possible to get in and out, at least on minor roads.

It was difficult to bring the details back to mind, Speer said. It was a long time ago, and one should also consider his own state of agitation. As far as he can recall, Hitler also expressed a mixture of respect and contempt for Britain, although he has forgotten the actual words. Then Hitler spoke of the unexpected strength of the Russians, which he had for a long time underestimated, and about the Germans, whom he had overestimated for too long. Those were probably the 'two principal mistakes of his life'. For a long time he had not wanted to see them. Now he was giving in. It was easy for him to leave this life; death was just one ridiculous second, a tiny moment. Then he puffed out his cheeks and emitted a scornful sound. In a conclusive gesture, he threw his metal-rimmed glasses down on the table. After some rather forced pondering, Speer said he could not tell us any more.

He picked up the thread again a little later and said that he had heard only individual key phrases. While Hitler had spoken in fits and starts, in a remarkably jerky manner, he (Speer) had more and more followed his own thoughts. This was another reason why his memory was so inadequate, however irritating that might be for historians. As if to return to 'business', or to reality, he had raised during a pause in the conversation the matter of the Škoda directors who wanted to go 'to the West' – a wish that, to his surprise,

Hitler immediately granted. Speer then involuntarily reverted to his 'sombre mood', having naturally thought back to the common dreams that lay so far from the wilderness of rubble through which he had come. And, despite all the disputes between them in the past, he fell into a state of 'great emotion'.

Then, following some instinct much more than any definite purpose, he once again tried his reliable 'trick' and began to speak of the reconstruction of the cities, particularly the plans for Berlin, Munich and Nuremberg that had from time to time been carried further. But, presumably to offend him, Hitler soon turned the discussion to Linz and said that, a short time before, 'good old Giesler' had been to see him with revised plans. He had eventually referred Giesler to Fräulein Braun, who was entrusted with the development of the business district, promenades and parks of his native town; Fräulein Braun had made some 'very independent proposals' on the question. Speer was sure that Hitler used this expression purely to offend him. After all, years before he had himself offered to work on the Linz project. Now Hitler preferred Eva Braun.

Speer had not, however, observed any annoyance on Hitler's part. Probably his sentimental mood at the time was anyway too strong. And, of course, it also weighed with him that everything Hitler was talking about was sheer fantasy. What significance did Linz have now, or Berlin? Anyway, today he sometimes wonders whether the mixture of dejection and disgruntlement into which Hitler had fallen did not encourage him to bring up the real reason for his flight to the encircled Berlin, which had almost become lost in the course of the discussion and in the face of the pitiable old man. He felt a kind of 'compulsion to come out with it', but for a long time did not know what to say or how to formulate it without, as the secretaries said, getting him too worked up.

After several attempts, and actually in a haphazard way, he began to say to Hitler in a dry and husky voice that he had been defying the destruction order. For several months now. What had given him the courage – Speer said – was the thought that strictly speaking what he had to say was not a confession, since Hitler, as he now knows for certain, was fully in the picture. To head off the worst, he had had a hundred or more discussions with troops commonly loyal to the Party, and it was quite unthinkable that a few dozen of them had not informed Hitler (or, to be more precise, Bormann). So, after briefly pulling himself together, he told Hitler that for months he had not been able to follow the orders in question and, as far as possible, had suspended them.

To his astonishment, Hitler scarcely reacted to his revelation; he looked 'almost absent', and when they were again interrupted Speer did not quite know how to continue and added something about his enduring loyalty. He had the impression that Hitler was touched by these rather awkward words. In any case, he looked at him silently for a long time, and then some tears ran down his stiffened face. Although Speer had experienced a similar scene a couple of weeks before, he had to make every effort to retain his composure. He muttered something about his duty 'to spare the fatherland', but Hitler still said nothing and looked almost blankly at his gnawed fingertips.

To get beyond the terrible silence between them, he finally offered to remain with Hitler in Berlin. But Hitler looked past him into empty space. He gave the impression of having cut himself off from everyone, 'including me'. When he shortly afterwards went into the corridor, he saw the seated Ribbentrop still waiting there and looking distinctly uncomfortable. 'Almost as soon as he spotted me, he got worked up again over some question of protocol.' One room further on he came across the gigantic figure of

Dr Stumpfegger, Brandt's successor, and then Hewel, General Burgdorf and a few others. Von Below was there too.

That's all there is, Speer said. Everything else you already know.

▬▬▬ Afternoon. Speer adds to his account some details that he forgot to mention; the thing had been going round in his head and robbed him of his after-lunch rest. First, in the *Memoirs*, the murky concrete labyrinth, dimly lit by flickering bulbs, constantly gives off a terrible stench. On top of fire, sweat and rot came the stopped-up toilet pipes. It was indescribable: an underworld also in the transferred sense of Dante's inferno, as if it 'belonged to Hitler'.

This was not the least of the reasons why Hitler's birthday celebration, three days earlier, had taken place in the New Reich Chancellery. After the oppressive confinement of the deep bunker, the height and width of the rooms had had a liberating effect, and the mass of uniforms as well as the assiduously circulating SS orderlies in their white jackets had been one last touch that at least brought back the memory of past festivities, however remote all that was now from the largely empty halls and the floors studded in many places with splinters.

Around midday, Speer continued, an air raid – the last on Berlin, if he was not mistaken – had driven them once more into the shelters. But Hitler came back up only a few hours later. He looked very pale in the face and more frail than usual. His back seemed more bent, and the trembling in his left arm, however much he tried to hide it, was more noticeable than on all the previous days. Walking with difficulty, as if each step cost him a great effort, he first inspected the ad hoc ranks of those who had put in an appearance. Some lined up in the Winter Garden; as far as he can remember, Himmler, Bormann and Fegelein were among them, as well as von

Below. Later, when the discipline had relaxed a little, Hitler moved from group to group curiously expressionless, as if it was not the right moment, and received everyone's congratulations. 'Once I heard him say almost unintelligibly, more to himself, that there was no cause for congratulation.' The despondency was unmistakable on all sides.

When I asked what people had mostly talked about, Speer replied that, as is usually the case in hopeless situations, they escaped into trivia. Of course, there was talk of the decisive battle for Berlin looming ahead and of the, in one way or another, approaching end of the war. Memories were often conjured up to fill in the time: everyone had at some point experienced an apparently hopeless situation that then took a surprising turn for the better. 'Anyway, such is my faded recollection.'

The main impression that has stuck in his mind is that many people clung to the memory of better days. In reality, however, everyone wanted to get away as quickly as possible; the pair of ministry officials and the gauleiters displayed particular impatience for the reception to be over. Hitler's Luftwaffe adjutant, Nicolaus von Below, told him – without being able to vouch for it, of course – that Goering once instructed an orderly to find out how much longer the way south would remain open.

In the course of the event, Speer continued, Hitler's decision to divide the German armed forces between a 'North Staff' under Grand Admiral Dönitz and a 'South Staff' under Field-Marshal Kesselring was announced. At some point, when he was standing with Hewel, Schaub and one of the doctors working in the wider bunker precinct, Goebbels came in and praised Hitler's decision as 'a stroke of genius': the division of forces should not be seen as a sign of weakness; rather, the two groups should be regarded as the 'wings of one strategic pincer', which would soon close and deliver a 'second Cannae' to the unsuspecting enemy powers. He wondered whether Goebbels would trot out the same nonsense a few steps further on, where a couple of officers were standing in conversation, and whether he really believed what he said or needed it to raise his spirits.

The altogether modest court function did not last long, Speer said, because most of those giving the congratulations wanted to be out of the city. It occurred to him at one point, however, that Hitler might have sensed the general unease and therefore be spinning things out; he did have a thoroughly sadistic tendency. But later Speer said that Hitler, feeling wretched, may simply have wanted to delay for a few minutes the awarding of decorations to the Hitler Youth assembled in the garden and the beginning of the final situation conference with its string of horror reports.

On that day, incidentally, Hitler seemed to have half made up his mind to go to the 'South Staff'. Or anyway he was hesitating, and before or during the conference he again mentioned the Untersberg and its sleeping emperor. The view there, he said, had given him strength and confidence in many a seemingly hopeless situation.

===== A few more details from later in the afternoon. Before he went to see Hitler a second time, during the night of 24 April, there had been the uproar over Goering's telegram.[1] Bormann was again the 'real' Bormann, talking insistently to Hitler in half-sentences to wind him up against the Reich Marshal, who had anyway fallen out of favour. As he observed this, he (Speer) was half-amused but still more depressed that, although the Russians were at the gates, Bormann was still up to his intrigues. He could not do any different. Later he sometimes thought that Bormann was the truly authentic representative of the Reich: subaltern, ambitious, narrow-minded and duplicitous.

===== As night began to fall, on the road beyond the spa centre at Keitum, Speer returned once more to Hitler's unmistakable physical decline that had been advancing from day to day. Everyone was amazed that, during those days, his authority was undiminished, sometimes almost reinforced.

Hitler, Speer said, presented a pitiable figure. But now and then the thought crossed his mind that he was playing out his condition as a kind of role. He had always been so much an actor that he put on even his own infirmity. This may be what lay behind the repeated astonishment of Jodl, Krebs and even the old warhorse General Weidling, as well as other visitors from outside, when they spoke of 'the energy radiating' from Hitler (as Lüschen once put it).

Of course, Hitler knew that he was a wreck. But at the same time he used this condition, because a wreck looks more pitiable than someone full of strength and determination. And, as one could see, he had a lot of success with this conception, especially among the female staff in the bunker. Speer said that he would not express in public his suspicions about this last stage trick of Hitler's. He was talking of no more than a hypothesis that sometimes occurred to him. One should never forget that Hitler had been seriously ill for years. He thought it most likely that Hitler called attention to the frailty that caused him so much trouble, in order to impress people around him and to make them more yielding.

===== On the way back, along the Watt, Speer said that on the whole he has not sufficiently emphasized that he still thinks it was right and proper for him to return to Berlin to take his leave. Perhaps he has also not made it clear enough that Hitler was the key reason for his decision to return to the city; he had not wanted to stay away. Then, constantly faltering, he said: 'After years of common plans and somehow also friendship, I could not act for months against his

The Great Gallery/Long Hall in the Speer-designed New Reich Chancellery in Berlin, before its destruction

orders and then simply make myself scarce. With a lie, to boot! I would have despised myself for the rest of my life.'

====== 'And one more thing', he said. He had also wanted to make it clear to Hitler that, with his 'scorched earth' policy, he had lifted the spell in which he had held him all those years. That was something else Hitler should know. And also that this had 'wounded or even destroyed' their friendship and what it had been based upon. All this, as well as other motives, had come together in his decision. He did not know which of them had been the strongest.

====== In answer to the point that he had put his life in danger by returning to Berlin, and that this had also affected his family, Speer later said: 'Yes, the family – I have to hold that against myself. But so many things were pulling on me.' By the way, he had not felt afraid the whole time – not so much because he was particularly courageous as because many other things had been more important at that moment. After all, for years he too had expected millions of people to give their lives, and death from a Russian anti-aircraft gun might even have been a 'more fitting end' for him.

In any event, he had been far more concerned about how Hitler would behave. He was not at all sure that he would let him get away with it. There was the cautionary example of Karl Brandt, who had also belonged to Hitler's inner circle and, so it was said, had been sentenced to death simply for sending his family from Berlin 'too early' and, despite Hitler's offer, not to the 'Mountain' but to Thuringia, 'to the Americans'. Kaufmann, the Hamburg gauleiter, had also told him that he would not at all rule out a death sentence, since Hitler, as everyone had seen on countless occasions, was unpredictable. Strangely enough, however, he did not draw any conclusions at that time. 'It's just death, that's all', he said to himself over and over again.

Nevertheless, I retorted, it was a truly crazy decision that did not at all fit in with his general calmness and prudence. I accepted that he had had no fear of a kind of soldier's death. But to be condemned by a vengeful man of unsound mind, someone he himself regarded as a 'madman' and deliberate destroyer of the country: that amounts to a suicidal impulse. Had he been prepared to put an end to his life? Or simply to chuck it in because of the hopelessness of the situation?

Speer gave it some more thought, then said: 'No, not suicide. More a wild fatalism, if there is such a thing.' One has to keep the circumstances in mind. What was happening was the end of a world, quite literally. And he had always been susceptible to the grandeur of the hour, even one like that. Still today, looking back from a great distance, he thinks it right that he did not simply make off. 'At the same time I accepted death. But there was no more to it.' When I persisted and said with perhaps a trace of irony that he might have been driven by something like a Wagnerian yearning, in which only death can set the seal on everything great and important in man, he replied abruptly and a little condescendingly that I had evidently not shaken off my 'stereotypes'.

===== (*Addendum in the late evening to today's discussion.* Speer says that, although he did not think of suicide in those final days, life no longer had any appeal to him. He often reads that he is supposed to have done this or that to save his own skin. But, whether one believes it or not, that was the last thing in his mind. Anyway, most of them had been so infected by the regime and the mood of the times that they attached 'virtually no importance to life'. He too, evidently. Strange how difficult it is for today's affluent citizens to grasp that, he added. No one accepts it when he says it. But all those who thought 'idealistically' were of the same view. He was by no means an exception, as historians at least should be able to judge. 'Why does anyone become a historian', he added, 'if they can't find the will or the capacity to empathize with those who lived in the past?')

===== The fact that Hitler had his friend Karl Brandt sentenced to death and, so it was rumoured, personally demanded 'the most severe consequences' made it clear to Speer what an evil man Hitler was. Moreover, all the accusations against Brandt also applied to himself, from the fact that he had sent his family to safety 'in the West' right through to the fact that, possibly more than Brandt, he had been distinguished by 'the Führer's friendship'. But, in the confusion of those weeks, he did not give the matter much thought. Only after his return from encircled Berlin did it occur to him how much he had been in danger. Then he already began to wonder why Hitler had let him get away with it.

A few days before, in a surge of emotion, he had spoken in Hitler's antechamber of making some attempt to get Brandt released, and had actually asked for the address of the Berlin villa where he was being held. He thinks it was Frau Schröder who called him to order with a raised finger. 'Herr Speer! Don't go too far! At some point the Führer's patience also runs out.'

Of course he was being extremely foolhardy, Speer added, and he made things still worse by asking Frau Schröder to treat what she had heard confidentially. One could scarcely have behaved in a more treasonable manner. He was lucky that Frau Schröder did hold her tongue.

===== Speer says he has already mentioned the breakdown of discipline during his visit of 23 April to the bunker, but it had already begun some time before. For example, one came across people smoking cigarettes in the outer bunker or even on one of the upper steps leading to the garden exit – which would previously have been inconceivable. In some rooms half-empty bottles were lying around, and discarded coats or jackets were hanging on coat hooks. All very abnormal.

To be sure, one other thing was even more striking. When Hitler passed a room, it was unusual for one of the people sitting there to stand up. Many acted as if they had not noticed him and even went on talking, especially as Hitler generally did not glance at them but, as if lost in thought, walked past with an outstretched hand looking for the support of a wall or piece of furniture. It also happened that one of the orderlies addressed him as 'Herr Speer' instead of with one of his official titles.

===== He has sometimes wondered why, on the day after his farewell visit, Hitler agreed to the proposal to take down 'my candelabra on the east–west axis'.[2] Perhaps he meant this to be 'one last kick in the teeth'. For the opportunity had gone to have him shot, Speer added with a little laugh.

In any event, von Below believed that the intention had been to get even with Speer. Von Below told him not long ago that Hitler had been almost 'wrought up' giving his approval when he, Below, had said that certain pilots wished to take down the street lighting because it would improve their conditions for taking off and landing. However, Speer thinks this interpretation exaggerated. It should also be considered, he said, that there was massive confusion in the confined, always overcrowded storage room; who on earth knew what things were like in Hitler's head?

====== After some questions and answers about this and that, Speer added that, before Hitler's fit of rage on hearing that Steiner's relief attack had not taken place, he sent the crowd of people there out of the conference room and shut the door. But, in the course of the fit, someone evidently opened it again – whether for a short or long time, he does not know. In any event, as far as he remembers, von Below, Stumpfegger and Rattenhuber gave him the impression that they had not only heard what was going on, like many others crowded round, but in part had followed the scene with their own eyes: how Hitler beat his fists against his temples, gesticulated and once even broke into sobbing; how he pointed an accusatory arm at some unnamed traitor and finally left the room.

Speer thought that you don't tell such things, or anyway not how they were done, unless you were a direct witness. He says this, he added, because at Nuremberg Keitel replied to a question of his on the subject by claiming that no one apart from the few people in the conference room – Jodl, Burgdorf, Krebs and a few others – were present when Hitler made his unprecedented entrance, and that therefore only they can present themselves as witnesses. Keitel himself, and a few others subsequently, tried to have a face-to-face conversation with Hitler soon after his exit and to persuade him that he should open negotiations, preferably from Berchtesgaden. But Hitler rejected everything and replied that he would stay in Berlin and conquer – or go to his death as 'a symbol of the National Socialist idea' and a 'guarantee of its survival'. By the way, Speer added, Keitel still appeared quite indignant that during his fit Hitler had especially called the officer corps 'a gang of traitors and failures'.

===== In the *Memoirs*, Speer said, he described his visit to Eva Braun and how she impressed him with her stoical, almost philosophical composure. But he did not mention how much everyone there had been infected with the bacillus of mutual suspicion. For, once in the course of the 'spirited chat' with which Eva Braun tried to gloss over the situation, she suddenly asked where 'his wife and children' were, and for a moment it occurred to him that she wanted to find out so that she would be able to threaten him with the fate of Dr Brandt.

He managed to stutter something in reply, but before he could say anything more precise she moved on to something else and expressed her joy that he had returned and was again with her. Several times in the past few days she had heard it suggested that Speer was disloyal and no different from all the others whom the Führer had distinguished with his friendship. She firmly believed that the suspicions had all originated with Bormann, but she had always contradicted them. Now she was glad she had been proved right.

When he left Eva Braun, it occurred to him how many common experiences they had had and how much their friendship in all the past years had rested on them: 'Both she and I, so to speak, had fallen under Hitler's hypnotic power.

We suffered because of him, hated him at times, yet were not able to free ourselves of him.'

═════ He also spoke a few words with Eva Braun about Magda Goebbels, Speer continued. For a while, especially during their marital crisis on account of Lida Baarova, he had after all been one of her confidants. In all their meetings he got to know her as an emotionally strong woman with an occasional tendency to sentimentality, for whom her own children were everything. For this reason he never understood her decision to take the children into the bunker. For, of course, he had known what that meant. Everybody did.

At first he still thought, or anyway talked himself into thinking, that she wanted to be with the others in the shelter of the 'bunker hell'. But it soon became clear that the children had been brought there to die. That required a coldness and callousness that he had never attributed to her. No one with whom he later discussed it was able to understand it either.

Not only Hitler, and at first Goebbels himself, tried to talk her out of it. Apart from the top generals, who were too stiff and formal for such things, almost everyone from Hitler's inner circle tried to get her to change her mind. Even Krebs, Hewel and Linge. So too did Bormann, or at least so Eva Braun told him during his final visit, although she also expressed a suspicion that Bormann had only done so to engineer a common exit from the bunker. For, until literally the last minute, he had continued to hope for an escape from the 'death trap', as the bunker was colloquially described in those days. 'Off to the mountains!' said Eva Braun, in the sporty style she sometimes adopted. That was where he had wanted to go; then everything else would sort itself out. But Magda Goebbels had remained firm even with Bormann, and as time went by her refusal to take the children away became visibly more impatient and finally even curt. Eva Braun ended her remarks about Magda Goebbels with the words: 'What on earth got into her? Or have we all become so unfeeling and inhuman?'

When he heard these words, Speer said, he must have thought of the visit he had just made to the sick, bedridden Magda Goebbels. But he had made no attempt to dissuade her from her plans, since all the time Goebbels was standing just behind him and registering his every word.

───── Most fortunately, Speer said, Friedrich Lüschen – who was one of his closest friends – came to the Reich Chancellery to say farewell to him. They were 'warm moments', he said, with one of those slightly gauche expressions that kept slipping out when he spoke of anything to do with feelings. When he reached the exit, accompanied by Hitler's SS adjutant Otto Günsche, he said by way of farewell: 'Don't get too worried, Günsche. I'll send a couple of Fieseler Storchs to get you out of here.'[3] Günsche answered with a brief bow. But not one word.

───── I asked Speer why on earth, after his safe return flight from Berlin, he had gone to see Himmler in Hohenly-chen of all places. He said that he had heard in Rechlin that it was impossible to fly on to Hamburg because of the numbers of British fighters in the skies above the city; he would have to wait until evening.

To spend a whole day in pointless waiting seemed a terrible idea at that time. He could have retired somewhere, of course, but whatever he did would have been dangerous. Then there was the business with Dr Brandt, which he wanted to talk about with Himmler. And he also wanted to know whether the SS Reichsführer had finally cast off his arrogance. 'I wanted to see him tremble, like Bormann just before.' But Himmler disappointed him, he remembers, and his wish was fulfilled only a fortnight later, when he refused his and Colonel Baumbach's request for an aircraft with which to escape. It is true that Himmler still acted the 'great man', but he was visibly gripped with fear and for the first time the always curiously lifeless 'marionette' could be seen shaking. 'Special needs I had at the time, what do you think?' he concluded.

━━━━ I told Siedler, who only arrived today, about Speer's account of the final visit to the bunker. Not without sarcasm he expressed his satisfaction that Speer was at least now, considerably later, coming out with such details.

Then about the reasons why Speer may have been so laconic about the farewell to Hitler (and much else besides). For the whole episode, including the declaration of loyalty before they parted, was not more compromising for him than many other things with which he had dealt thoroughly. Does he think that the event was too melodramatic? Or that it betrayed too much sentiment?

Siedler said that after all it had been the end of a love affair, and no one wants to see that broadcast to the whole world, least of all an emotionally blocked person like Speer. But the real farewell, I replied, was the fit of crying that came over Speer in Flensburg. And he recorded that in the *Memoirs* without such fine inhibitions. We agreed to question him about it one more time.

━━━━ In the evening with Siedler about how 'crazy' or, to say the least, 'terribly juvenile' was Speer's decision to visit the Reich Chancellery again for a 'completely personal' farewell, three days after the semi-official leave-taking on Hitler's birthday. Everything he brought up about his need to confess his 'betrayal' to Hitler sounded unbearably kitschy in a 'German' sort of way. A deep friendship should not end in deception, a breach of trust or another kind of 'baseness', Speer had explained with a look of intense emotion. Never in the past, I said, had I felt so distant from Speer as during this honest and horrifying admission. For the sake of a criminal of unsound mind, he had not only put his life at risk but suppressed all thought of his family – and lurking in the background had been a long since hollow concept of trust that Hitler himself had betrayed innumerable times. What kind of a world had Speer been living in? I asked Siedler. And, as I told him, I had asked Speer the same thing at the end. Speer had flashed back that awkward smile of an initiate and said: 'That's something you can't understand!' He was certainly right about that.

====== During our late evening stroll, Siedler asked whether I had again tried to find out what had earlier prevented Speer from reporting the details of his farewell visit to Hitler and why he had betrayed so much emotion in recalling that last meeting. I told him of Speer's terse and unusually cool, almost reproachful, explanation: 'Why do I have to tell you over and over again that I simply hadn't wanted to, and that I still think my decision was right?'

We considered whether he had something to hide and why he might be acting in this way. For a moment we discussed the suspicion that Speer returned to the bunker not so much to make his intended 'confession' as to find out what chances he had of succeeding Hitler. But we soon dismissed the idea. Too much spoke against it.

====== Next day. Hoping to relieve our ignorance, I asked Speer straight out why he had never described the farewell visit of all things and always refused to accept our requests. On the note about it that I rediscovered only a day or two ago, it is recorded that Speer had said with an impatient gesture of dismissal: 'Very personal!' And then almost angrily: 'Too personal!' I still wonder what that meant.

══════ Later, in a review of our work with Speer, Siedler said that he wanted to put aside the moods of slight resignation that had appeared in the last few days; we had, all in all, got a lot out of Speer that he had originally been unwilling to make public. He concluded ironically that his own charm plus my severity were an 'irresistible mixture'. Nevertheless, I replied, Speer had resisted our question about how much he knew of the crimes. 'If he knew of them', Siedler came in. But he added that he too found it difficult to believe Speer on that score.

══════ Speer had to do something and returned in the afternoon. As we walked along the beach, Siedler got him to outline once more how things had gone during the final visit to the bunker. The question as to why it is dismissed with such arid words in the *Memoirs* drew forth Speer's enigmatic, somewhat supercilious smile. But no answer. Similarly, Siedler's proposal to include a report on it in the *Spandau Diaries* elicited from Speer no more than a negative shake of the head.

When we returned to the hotel, Speer suddenly said that perhaps Hitler spared him and let him escape with his life because he 'had spent the happiest days of his life with me'. The question of whether the reverse was true suggested itself too strongly for us not to put it to ourselves after Speer had gone to his room. But we were also sure that he would not have answered it.

══════ Speer spoke of the stupidity with which even top officers tried to talk their way out of their duty to obey during the days of the collapse. This was never clearer to him than at the end of April 1945, following his farewell visit to the Reich Chancellery, when he went from Hamburg to the nearby headquarters of Field-Marshal Ernst Busch to talk him out of the senseless plan to blow up the docks and harbour installations. Busch was only indignant that Speer, together with gauleiter Kaufmann, had rescinded the orders without informing him that they had done so. 'What are things coming to!' Busch complained, shaking his head in a troubled way. Manstein, who also happened to be there, asked if it had been done 'deliberately against the Führer's orders', and when Speer said 'yes' Busch threw in, as if he had great difficulty grasping such an enormity: 'Really? Is that true?' When Speer then stood his ground and referred to the sufferings of the population, to the catastrophe for hundreds of thousands that would result if the explosions went ahead, and finally to the end of hostilities just around the corner, they both repeated in chorus: 'Really?! Against the Führer's orders?' And they looked at each other as if they had seen a kind of apparition, as if the world were collapsing right before their eyes.

Never had the character weakness of leading officers been so clear to him as at that moment. 'It was as if they were suddenly standing there naked.' Again and again Busch shook his head in bewilderment: 'Just like that. You and Kaufmann used your own discretion?' And then, as a result of his pondering: 'Nothing good will come of it, Speer!'

When he heard that and thought of the devastation resulting not least from the blind obedience they still advocated, he said goodbye and left. Anything further would have seemed pointless. 'Our parting was very formal.'

===== Speer said he would like to speak again to the British sergeants who had stormed up the stairs in Glücksburg, past the soldiers on guard and the castle staff, and called out in English: 'Who is Speer?' He would also dearly like to know what it had meant when, before leaving the room, the man had unfastened his gun belt and placed it before him on the table.

8

TRIAL, PRISON YEARS, RELEASE

Merano, November 1974. Today, when we came to the Nuremberg trial, Speer maintained what he had said several times before: that he had definitely been expecting a death sentence, especially after the showing of the horrific film from the camps. Those pictures taken by the Americans robbed him of any possibility of a defence. The same applied to the report by a German engineer (Friedrich Gräbe) that Shawcross quoted in his summing up. When asked why he had nevertheless fought so hard for his life, he gave it some thought and replied that it was possible only if you resolutely suppressed such things. And then, in the nonchalant manner with which he liked to smooth over critical situations: 'Besides, I was also guided by sporting motives.' He knew the expression was inappropriate. But he had not so much escaped with his life as simply not wanted to lose it. And after a pause: 'Whatever his guilt, can you really blame someone for defending himself, so long as it is not at someone else's expense?'

====== We asked Speer about the remarkable 'fit of weeping' that came over him in the last days of the war as he was unpacking his trunk in Flensburg. After all, months earlier he had described Hitler as a 'criminal', contravened his orders and even contemplated an attempt on his life. We wanted to know something about the character of his feelings for Hitler. But he would not be drawn and gave the impression of being surprised, as if he felt the question was foolish or illegitimate. At that time he had not yet been 'finished' with Hitler, which meant with his own life, he said abruptly. And with that he again pulled down the 'blinds', as we called them.

To the further question as to when, in that sense, he was 'finished' with Hitler, he became embarrassed and gave a shrug: he was unable to say. And, when Siedler pressed him as to whether he was completely over him some twenty-five years later, Speer reacted with a momentary confusion. 'Today that's all over', he finally said; 'politically, it has been for a long time.' His question had surprised Speer with the truth, I told Siedler, as I had done several times before, when we were alone.

====== The next morning, Speer about his relationship with Hitler. One should not forget that their relationship was not exclusively political. Many saw only self-interested motives at work: big contracts, an exceptional career. But that was a mistake. There had also been emotions. But who – he said in essence – can describe the causes of his emotions, their beginning, their strength and their disappearance, as if it were an arithmetical problem?

Later, Speer came back to the subject. Perhaps the 'final turning point', as he had repeatedly stressed, was the showing of the film in Nuremberg, shortly after the opening of the proceedings. It greatly distressed him and deadened the few remaining feelings. From then on, he was not able to see a

Speer at the witness stand of the International Military Tribunal in Nuremberg, 1946

death sentence as unjust. When asked again why he had nevertheless put up such a passionate defence, he seemed taken aback and said: 'Maybe because, apart from what has already been said, it again gave me a task to carry out. Also, you well know that I'm incapable of "doing things by halves".'

===== Early on he entered into long-term conflict with his fellow prisoners, he said. Nearly all of them thought that his willingness to talk to the Allies was 'dishonourable'. Such accusations meant nothing to him, he said, coming as they did from 'another world'. But, when he thinks about it, the prediction was true that he would do damage to himself. One day, at the Kransberg internment camp, Schacht had raised a warning finger: 'You'll carry things so far that you'll end up before the court!'

Schacht was right in the end, Speer added, and perhaps his talkativeness really had been ill-considered. 'But he, who didn't say a word "of his own free will", went there with me.'

====== On the Nuremberg trial. At the beginning he had been rather calm, but as the proceedings developed a growing (and, by the end, great) nervousness came over him. He had never been able to understand why most of his co-defendants kept talking of the illegitimacy of the proceedings. When Jackson, the chief American prosecutor, conceded at the beginning that the tribunal had a certain formal weakness, some in the dock immediately started crowing, as if this meant that the actual crimes had been conjured away. He had a brief and angry, but quite fruitless, argument with Dönitz. When Speer proved incorrigible, Dönitz turned away and said no more.

Until the run-up to the trial he had been on almost friendly terms with Dönitz. But he could feel all that collapse at the moment of the scornful brush-off. 'He won't be the only one to go a different way, I said to myself as I gazed after him.'

====== Dönitz was also the most difficult of his fellow prisoners during the Spandau years; they started quarrelling whenever they exchanged a few words. Any attempt to avoid acrimony proved vain. The arguments began over the 'total responsibility' Dönitz had taken over, and they by no means ended with Speer's moral acceptance of the verdict. He once accused Speer of slandering not only the internees but the whole German people, and said that he had 'forgotten his honour'. Evidently that is what they all thought.

====== Speer talked about the statements made by the head of Einsatzgruppe D, Otto Ohlendorf, and then about the report by engineer Hermann Friedrich Gräbe; the evidence shook him so much that he several times thought of killing himself. His life, he said to himself, was anyway over, and through his suicide perhaps 'a visible signal' could be given. Despite all the contradictory experiences, he had always believed in the great, idealistic side of their rule and considered the corruption, duplicity and egoism at the top to be an expression of human weaknesses that occur everywhere. Only in Nuremberg did he see how erroneous that belief had been.

======= With Speer about his closing remarks at Nuremberg, in which he recalled not without a sense of satisfaction that he had rid himself of all petty personal viewpoints and looked at the broader context. I objected that, contrary to what he claimed at the time, the Hitler regime had not been a demonstration of the consequences resulting from technology, and that I detected in his testimony more the *Wandervogel* of old.

Of course, the mass crimes of the rulers would not have been conceivable without the technological means to commit them. But technology cannot be guilty on principle. Rather, it was people sitting at desks and wielding instruments who had committed the atrocities. In the end, the building of concentration camps and the operation of gas chambers was not a problem of technology.

Speer's contradiction showed how difficult it was for him to give up that way of seeing things. In the end, he said that not the least of the reasons for his concluding remarks had been a wish to exonerate the German people. Lengthy discussion about whether he had been right to argue 'tactically'. Speer said it should not be forgotten that he was standing before a victor's court. As to whether he would have behaved differently before a German court, he could give no convincing answer.

Speer (standing) makes his final statement to the International Military Tribunal in Nuremberg, 31 August 1946.

====== On the accusation that he manipulated the judges and won over the prosecutors with a few tricks. How can a defendant be blamed for trying to win the courtroom battle? In reality, he did not incriminate anyone, not even Sauckel, in a way that went contrary to the truth. In the end, the will to survive is an overpowering instinct. He too wanted to 'save' himself, even if he never knew why. Later, especially in Spandau, he often thought he would have done better to give up all resistance.

When the court finally handed down its verdict, Speer continued, he was naturally relieved at first. But this was more a brief satisfaction at 'success in the duel' than a feeling that he had received back as a present the life already given up for lost – a feeling that one felt even in the face of a twenty-year prison sentence. When he went to his cell, the eerie quiet struck him for the first time, and fear of how he would cope with the twenty years welled up inside him. Was the sentence not a far worse punishment than the gallows? He expressed his despair to his wife, who was allowed to visit him at that time: 'What shall I begin to do with all these years ahead? Do they not come down to a permanent death sentence starting anew each day?' As his wife later told him, he used to whisper that in the middle of enquiring after his parents or the children and how they were coping with life.

What helped him most was another thought. Throughout his life he had been lucky enough to find an answer to all crises, troubles and difficulties, some task to do, some challenge or job. The twenty-year sentence handed down by the court had blocked that way out. For the first time in his life, he was denied the solution to a serious predicament. 'That was what deeply depressed me.'

━━━━━ Still today, Speer said, he is glad that he learned only towards the end of his imprisonment in Spandau that every evening the custodial powers threw everything the prisoners had written into the shredder. It is true that, when his notes of the day were collected, he usually handed over only copies of his letters to Wolters or his family. But also, on many occasions, there were thoughts, mementoes or impressions from his reading, which he hoped to get back after his release. All that is irretrievable.

Writing was for him quite literally a 'survival aid'. If he had known at the beginning of the twenty years that everything would be destroyed, he would undoubtedly not have pulled through. He felt as a result of communication like the rider on Lake Constance. If he had been told before, and if he had not had his friendly smuggler, he would have fallen through the ice.

When asked what he meant by this, Speer replied casually, almost without thinking: 'Precisely what I say: I would have put an end to it. I anyway got close to that several times in Spandau.'

═══ Early December 1974. Among his papers he found a note that dates more or less from the final months in Spandau. It says that he will never solve the mystery of his life. It's true that he was guilty, was branded a criminal, sentenced and so on. But what was the alternative in terms of his life as a whole? Should he have preferred to spend the autumn of his life as a town planning adviser in Göttingen, looking back as an architect at the buildings of the municipal savings bank or the local swimming pool? That's more or less what he wrote there.

We persuaded Speer to include these thoughts in the text. This time with success. But Speer said he still needed to work on the little note stylistically. Besides, it also says that he felt a kind of dizziness when he thought about the two paths that his life could have taken. For evidently the difficulty of answering this question is something like the key problem of his existence. He is still not in a position to solve it.

A lot more about this. 'You see', Speer concluded the discussion, 'there is no end to the questions.' And at the very end: but what would he do without such problems? Then it really would come down to his being the town planning adviser in Göttingen. He has no problems. Certainly not that kind, anyway.

═══ A slightly remorseful-sounding call from Speer. He reminded me how indignant he had been when I had not wanted to drop the 'suicide idea' supposedly driving him into his final visit to the Reich Chancellery. In any event, he has found among the Spandau papers a note that half confirms

The fortifications of Spandau prison, with its watchtower and guard posts. In the prison yard is Albert Speer.

my suspicion. In it he regrets that Hitler did not order a firing squad when they parted, and says that this would have been the 'best ending' to his life. All in all, he concluded, the note points to exactly what I claimed to have been the case.

I replied that my remark had not been very original, simply what immediately suggested itself. Later, Speer said that I should take into account that the note was probably written in the throes of one of the many Spandau depressions. He was not at all sure that the thought of death, or even, as I assumed, a longing for death, had then had him in its grip. Rather not, he thinks.

═══ Speer's recent calls have again given me a sense that he is looking for encouragement. He evidently feels very cut off from the world and from people. Today he more or less said that he has upset everyone. Some blamed him for a kind of enslavement to Hitler for far too long, while others accused him of having 'betrayed' him. Furthermore, everyone speaks of his 'machinations', of his 'calculation' or 'cunning' – as if his whole life has consisted of calculations and the pursuit of advantage. Even well-meaning people did not believe his regrets. He spoke of 'distrust on all sides'.

Perhaps he suffers more from being excluded than he cares to admit. But then he says that in the end he chose this condition and must now put up with it. He has neither a talent for nor an inclination to self-pity. Right at the end, however, in a slightly interrogatory tone: was I also of the opinion that he had not acquitted himself wrongly?

===== February 1975. The second manuscript also nearly finished. To round it all off, more or less, again on Sylt. Speer has the, so to speak, literary problem of describing the everyday monotony of twenty years' imprisonment without becoming too monotonous himself. Instead, he must switch to the 'internally' unfolding drama, which resolved itself in a surprising way. To avoid breaks between entries, all that is really necessary is to make a few excisions or to introduce a few linking ideas.

Speer is having considerable trouble, however, with the book's conclusion, and I advised him to invoke the recurrent dream of recent years that he has reported several times. The sequence is always the same, he said. He sees himself, sometimes in prison clothes, standing directly before the massive gate of Spandau prison and asking to go back to his cell after the disappointment of freedom. When the wardens deny him access, he has said once or twice, he asks to see the governor. But he too merely shakes his head and sends him away with an indulgent gesture.

'Yes', Speer confirmed, that recurs more and more often in his dreams. And recently the governor sometimes even smiles, as if he thinks he is disturbed. Perhaps, Speer continued, he can't cope with a free life. And finally, he added, the strange dream also reveals how he turned to Hitler and one of his motives for it.

====== Walking beside the sea down to Westerland, we again talked of the literature that Speer read in Spandau and then of the theological books with which he struggled.

He finds metaphysical thinking very difficult, but at least a kind of peace radiates from it. Altogether he has certainly read several thousand pages of theology. When asked which ideas or which book he remembers as having been especially helpful, he became unsure of himself, knitted his brow and finally acknowledged that he could not name anything specific. No ideas? we asked. After pondering over it, he shook his head almost sadly. 'Let's drop it', he said, 'everything would anyway sound false in my mouth.'

====== On the same walk Speer spoke, as more than once before, of the deep disappointment of the family reunion in early October 1966. In Spandau he had been constantly worried that he would lose his connection with his family, and for a time he even feared that he had lost it already. Of course there had been the pathetic meetings that they took it in turns to have with him in the visitors' room, and each time, however short the meeting, he had been tired by the play-acting that it demanded of him. The whole time he had to pretend for them to be the semi-composed and self-assured prisoner, but 'that was not what I was'. An 'architect in a structure of lies' is what he used to call himself then.

Perhaps, Speer added, it may have been that very experience which made him so awkward when they saw each other again after his release. He blames no one but himself for the fiasco.

In fact, he said to himself, it was probably inevitable that things went badly; too many hopes rested on it. Anyway he felt much more alone during those days than he had ever done in Spandau, and to his horror, amid the forced gaiety of the togetherness, he found himself wishing that he was back in his cell – this time 'wide awake', not in a dream.

Equally unfortunate were the so-called conventions of his former colleague Theodor Hupfauer. Terrible how, among all those old friends and close colleagues seated there, and at their request, he began to speak about Hitler, armaments, disputes with the ever wounded Goering or with Kammler, and of course the good qualities of one or another of those present and the ways in which they had distinguished themselves. But it soon became clear to him that everything he said was falling on deaf ears, that there was nothing less that the assembled company wanted to hear than old stories of that kind.

Everyone was friendly and tried hard, he said, but nothing of what he said interested them. As far as they were concerned, it was all out of a different and remote past. When the workshop discussions got under way, people immediately began to speak of their current affairs and truly remarkable successes, and sometimes it occurred to him that he must have been the same in the old days. It was an exceptionally inverted or time-warped picture that offered itself to him at those gatherings, and he quickly recognized: 'I was just in the way.' There was only one embarrassing situation of this kind. Significantly enough, Speer added, the 'conventions' soon stopped happening.

===== During one of our daily walks on the Watt, I asked Speer about the occasional claim that, as the pushy and unscrupulous individual that many saw in him, he was already planning his post-war career by the end of 1944 (at the latest). The resistance to the 'scorched earth' policy, the assassination plan and so on should be seen as mere attempts to create an alibi for himself. Speer came to a jerky halt and, clapping his hands together, shouted in a voice choking with amusement: 'Good Lord, whatever next?'

===== Speer quoted a saying of Nietzsche's that he recently read somewhere or heard from someone, in which he recognizes himself or the problem of his life. 'You cannot gaze long into an abyss without the abyss gazing into you.'[1] Something like that. It describes himself and his situation, he added.

===== Speer on the clichés in circulation about him. The problem is that they did not say the slightest thing to him. The more sensible ones he often found interesting, whether in history, the social world or psychological accounts, and they also made him upset. But he has to make quite an effort to relate them to himself. However perceptive they often sound, he recognizes in them nothing about himself and his life. He admires people such as Trevor-Roper or Bracher and others, even the certainly agreeable Herr Mitscherlich. But everything they have said strikes him as much too far-fetched.

He has always preferred people like John Kenneth Galbraith, who expressed briefly and sharply what he thought of a person's statements and roundly denied the credibility of the argument they made in their defence. 'I could argue that out.' But the picture of him as the 'real Nazi criminal' leaves him puzzled: not because of Trevor-Roper's accusation that he was guilty, but because of the tortuous ways of thinking by which he reached the accusation. Golo Mann stands 'on a different level', he added, before coming back once more to his review. He spoke of the mixture of 'astuteness, understanding and something like grief' that characterizes only a great historian.

===== Discussion with Siedler about the 'Speer automatic mechanism', as he called it: the almost mechanical confessions of guilt that he readily produces as if in response to a signal. Siedler sees in this something like Speer's lifelong feelings of superiority, though very encoded: Speer clearly wants to be first, even among sinners. I added that he knows how to live even with the guilt and has made himself at home in it. This makes it difficult, or even impossible, to get to know him.

But then we also recalled how the compulsion to accuse himself sometimes seemed to make him suffer. Everyone, he once complained, keeps asking about his guilt; obviously they wouldn't be able to come up with anything else. We spoke of his occasional statements to the effect that confessions of guilt mean nothing, are cheap to dish out and are at best only a beginning.

Anyway, he said, the real questions with which he has been wrestling begin only afterwards: how he became what he was, what life at home with his parents did to promote or discourage it, how one's reason can be blocked, how individuals or ideas can gain power over people, and what should be done to counter it. Or how one can go through life unmolested as a split personality, without even noticing the contradictions at the bottom of everything. A thousand questions. And why he, unlike many others, shook them off, despite a lot of internal and external resistance. Or how he has come to feel that the person he once was is a stranger, whom he would just pass by in the street without giving him a second glance.

But no one was interested in such questions, he complained; everyone kept their eyes fixed on his guilt. And now he plays along – he has to. Or, if a discussion immediately begins with that question, should he unceremoniously break it off? They were nice people who asked him, many of them young and naïve, like he himself was back in the early 1930s,

Speer with his wife on the way to a press conference, after his release from Spandau prison

when he saw all the students heatedly debating around him and said he would 'never dream' of joining a political party or even Hitler. But sometimes he had a suspicion that his questioners just wanted to feel morally superior.

===== More on the same subject. I reminded Siedler of something Speer said a while ago: one day he would surprise one of these interviewers by asking whether he had ever tried to found out how guilty Heinrich Mann felt, since he had not only condoned Stalin's mass crimes but defended himself with the verbal extravagance of a great writer. But Speer had added that such questions were obviously point-less, and further remarked that one could insert many con-temporary names in place of Stalin or Heinrich Mann. He also knew what would be said in reply: that he was pointing at others only to put himself in a somewhat better light and perhaps even to clear Hitler's name.

In a similar context, Siedler recalled, Speer said a while ago how reassuring it was that everyone with whom he had dealings was by now quite sure that they had not failed in anything during those years. Where did they all get their certainty from? Speer asked. Just as he had been, they too were 'cool', 'sober' and 'addicted' to their private interests rather than any other point of view: technocrats like himself, entrepreneurs, managers, office supervisors or whatever. What gave them the right to point their finger at him – especially those young prosecutors who are rising up all around? Are they just using the privilege of their shorter lives to be relatively guilt-free? Or has the disastrous habit of not looking beyond one's own horizon suddenly been broken?

Perhaps many really have learned something, Speer said when we raised some objections. And then, in the soft tone of an uncharacteristic disdain: this famously 'sceptical' generation has anyway learned not to have any doubts about itself. Hopefully this will not turn out some day to be the greatest failure, as it was in the case of his contemporaries. In any event, he wishes that today's young people will be spared the trials of his generation, when it was necessary to summon up greater discrimination and moral steadfastness, but also less fear of social exclusion and violence, than he had found possible.

===== On the last evening, Speer asked straight out why Hitler never gave him one of the potassium cyanide capsules that he so freely handed out on all sides. If he knew the reason, he said, he would also have an answer to the question about 'Hitler's real feelings for me'. In any case, he is convinced that Hitler did not simply forget to give him one of the ampoules; such things never happened. So, what could the reason have been?

We subsequently agreed that the question behind this question was why it was still important for Speer, a lifetime later, to require an explanation. With a hint of mockery, somewhat scornfully, we ended by saying that these were 'the inexplicable mysteries of a great love'.

===== On the return journey with Siedler: another review of Speer, our impressions, the historical richness of his two books, his repeatedly transparent inability to understand himself and the role he played in the apparatus of the Reich, which is evidently connected with his personality weaknesses, although it was precisely the 'personality' that enchanted everyone, and so forth. In the end, all we pieced together were contradictions. The man was hard to categorize, we said, but we thought this scarcely unusual, because historians must always be wary of applying 'pat' formulas to both individuals and circumstances. 'Writers too', Siedler said, and he again took the opportunity to heap ridicule on contemporary literature and its 'one-dimensional characters'. 'Siedler's cold barrage of derision', I once called it.

Siedler's attack led me to object that perhaps Speer's life did not unfold in the style of a novel showing its hero's formation or development: unhoped-for rise, years of radiance, fame and influence, then (after his appointment as minister) growing involvement in a colossal crime, and the final fall into imprisonment, recognition of guilt and troubled repentance.

Siedler remarked that Speer's life really did have some of the material for a classical *Bildungsroman*, but that no one would write it: not only because the 'flat-headed writers of today' would find it difficult to get to grips with such a broken figure, but also because, in the view of contemporary literati, a Nazi leader is not entitled to the semi-didactic, semi-elegiac tone always adopted in this genre.

══ I further pointed out that we probably underestimated the hunger for power that drove Speer once he had had a taste of it. He likes to present himself as the type of the purely task-driven manager. But that was much more the case with his predecessor, Todt. Speer was soon needing power as a drug and no longer wanted to give it up.

Later we talked about the loneliness from which Speer so evidently suffered, despite all his efforts to keep things secret. We wondered whether it was attributable simply to the disdain he encountered on all sides, or whether the lost drug of influence was not also plaguing him. Probably the lack of high-pitched tasks was another source of torment. Apart from the authorial work, he no longer dares to do much at all, even to express firm opinions.

Not long ago he spoke of the 'disqualifications' lying in wait around every corner. We wondered whether this is not the very reason why he is such a willing victim for all those people whom he once, in a surprising departure from his usual leniency, described as 'moral humdingers'.

EXPERT IN ESCAPES

March 1978. In London with Trevor-Roper. I asked him about the progress of the Speer project, but he parried by referring to his age and his need for an 'easy life'. When I expressed my dissatisfaction, he thought it over and said that other factors may also be involved; it was possible that he had been misled in the Speer case, because at the time, in Kransberg, he had judged him by comparison with the servile and contemptible 'clowns' from whose midst he suddenly appeared. They had all existed by virtue of power, or their proximity to power, and when the power was gone 'all that remained of their self-importance was the damp and limp balloon from which the air had escaped'. They were all 'men who revolted me by their abject behaviour'.

Against this background, Speer had undoubtedly cut an impressive figure; he had been intelligent, open and thoughtful, and fundamentally had not said anything untruthful. He should add, of course, that they had mostly left aside the moral issues, as he (Trevor-Roper) had mainly been concerned with the final days of the Nazi Reich. And at least in this respect, if his memory serves him right, Speer had displayed a remarkable distance from Hitler, the regime and everything that until the day before had been his own cause.

But years later, some time after Speer's release from Spandau, the BBC invited him to Munich for an interview. Together with John Kenneth Galbraith and George Ball, who soon after the war but still before the Nuremberg trial had also questioned Speer, he was supposed to interview him about all the issues thrown up by the Nazi regime and his role in it, 'revisited', as it were, twenty-five years on. 'Our task', Trevor-Roper said, 'was to put to him the questions that had not yet concerned us in 1945, and Speer was supposed to give the answers and to offer insights he had gained during the long years of imprisonment. This anyway was how Michael Charlton, the producer, had planned the programme and agreed it with those taking part.' He also admitted that he had looked forward with interest and even pleasure to the discussion. He immediately added, however, that the BBC never broadcast the programme, and he indicated that in the end the discussion had been rather a disappointment.

The changed picture that they all acquired, said Trevor-Roper, was due, in particular, to the scarcely comprehensible crimes that had lined the path of Hitler and his people until the end. The moral judgement overshadowing all memory of their rule therefore became a crucial issue. At some point in the interview, he asked Speer whether one might say that he, having been a member of the so-called war party (as he put it in the *Memoirs*), had had no reservations about Hitler's policy of aggression. In other words, was it correct that he had simply regarded the dictator as his construction client, who as the conqueror of Europe gave him the opportunity to build palaces, triumphal arches and other monuments across the whole continent? As he did before each of his answers, Speer thought for a moment and then simply said: 'Yes!' He uttered only that one careless, feeble word, and when Trevor-Roper asked if that was all he simply repeated: 'Yes!'

A little later in the discussion, Trevor-Roper reminded Speer that in the early summer of 1945 he had planned to escape to Greenland in his aircraft. Books, typewriter and many other objects were, according to his own written account, ready and waiting. Up there, away from the whole mess (he used the German word *Schlamassel*), he had intended to do some reading in peace, to draw and perhaps even to begin the memoirs he was already planning to write.

In the studio, Trevor-Roper continued, a somewhat longer discussion then ensued about the inhospitable climatic conditions in the far north. He remembers Speer literally saying: 'Oh, no, Greenland is simply wonderful in May and summer.' This remark first struck him not least because it revealed Speer's romantic tendency and showed him as the member of the Wandervogel youth association that he was all his life. But what would it have been like in winter? he asked. How had he intended to cope with that? 'Oh!' Speer replied, his idea had been to return to Germany in October. The war and all the horrors in its wake would by then surely be forgotten, and so he would be able to begin a new life 'in safety and comfort' based in Heidelberg.

Trevor-Roper had to confess that this rather shocked him. Perhaps Speer really believed it in 1945. 'But how could he simply come up with it again now, after Nuremberg and the twenty years of reflection in Spandau, without saying anything further to qualify it?' He would not rule it out that Speer had reacted oversensitively, or that he had simply been having a bad day. But he had suddenly felt a void open up behind all the intellectual sharpness and clarity. Speer was certainly not corrupt, nor malicious, hard-hearted, base or whatever. 'He was something far worse: hollow.' In an early article from the late 1940s, Trevor-Roper had ended by saying that Speer was in a sense 'the true criminal of Nazi Germany'. He had naturally been thinking of the well-known *trahison des clercs*. But he now wonders whether that was correct. For he doubts whether, after Munich, Speer had anything at all to betray.

I objected that in the final months of the war Speer did take a stand against Hitler's order to destroy everything, and that in doing this he risked his life dozens of times and – presumably not a slight matter for him – courted a shameful end. It should also be considered that, among the defendants at Nuremberg and later at Spandau, despite all the ostracization by those who shared his fate, he had stuck to his condemnation of Hitler's rule.

He had to accept that as evidence to the contrary, Trevor-Roper replied. But he still asked himself why Speer had acted in that way. In the name of which principles and standards had he remained so amazingly stubborn? Nor can he deny the injured feelings and even attacks of despair that it must have cost such an adaptation-hungry person as Speer to go 'his own peculiar way' and to live 'amid contempt' for so many years. It all added to the 'Speer mystery', about which he was already writing in the 1945 book.

Of course, he said later, it is no longer at all certain that we are talking of a distinctively German peculiarity or aberration. He often wonders what would have happened in Britain or France if Germany had won the First World War. One can speculate endlessly about that. But speculations are never an answer. At least he now knows that there is a problem here, which is far greater than the one man Speer, however enigmatic he may appear. It makes a biography of Speer extremely important. But probably not by him. He is too old for it. And anyway he hesitates too much. And then to me: why don't I write the book? It is not only the greatest challenge, but also the one with the greatest prospects: finally to provide an answer to the 'eternal question' of how Hitler was possible, and why precisely in Germany.

Next a lot more about Germany and Britain, especially the differences: the 'myth' of the great charismatic man in the former, the 'myth' of the constitutional, venerable institutions in the other. Then about the nineteenth century, 'the great century for the Germans', as Trevor-Roper put it, when they were the 'cultural dynamo' in Europe, with the most exceptional minds and the highest standards of education – and how everything 'promptly and silently' fell apart, almost enthusiastically surrendered in the face of an openly barbaric mass movement with a 'great man' at the top.

He thinks that this defection, especially of the elites, goes back more or less to the position of prime importance that the country had formerly occupied. The Germans sparkled for too long intellectually and culturally. In their 'secret extremism' they suddenly grew tired of that kind of grandeur. They were then gripped by what they call, in a superb and untranslatable word, *Erkenntnisekel*.[1] This opened many doors, and Hitler then walked through them. But, Trevor-Roper concluded, this and many other differences that made Europe colourful, terrible and great are now passing away, under the pressure of the global society.

Later, departure. As we said goodbye, Trevor-Roper pressed me once more about the Speer biography. I countered that it was now his affair. But he shook his head: he most regrets the title he thought up for the project, which was supposed to be about *Parsifal* and the 'coldness' of feeling. A kind of epigraph or heading already exists for the final chapter: 'Ignorant through Calculation'.[2] For a moment Trevor-Roper looked thoughtfully ahead, as if he nevertheless regretted giving up the project. 'Sorry!' he said, with a shrug. Now, an hour after we parted, I am wondering whether he did not give it up long ago.

===== May 1978. A call from Speer in Koblenz, where he is working at the Federal Archives. He asks whether I still remember the speech by Saur[3] which I once showed him years ago, during our work on the *Memoirs*. He had to give me a helping hand, but then it came back to me that I had indeed discovered somewhere an uncommonly coarse and repulsive speech by his deputy to employers in the arms industry. When I asked him whether he had ever expressed himself so disgracefully in public, he read the piece and assured me in a tone of deeply wounded gravity that that was not his style. Saur had been a primitive guy, who was actually quite proud of his primitiveness. Nothing like that would be found among his own papers.

Today he said that he had to take that back. There are a few speeches in which he expressed himself, at least in passing, in a similarly brutal manner. When he was looking through his papers in the Federal Archives, he came across an Albert Speer he had obviously thoroughly repressed. He wonders to what extent the period, the regime and, of course, power alienated him from himself.

===== (*Addendum*. During a later visit to Frankfurt, Speer brought me three passages of text and presented them with an almost schoolboyish awkwardness. The point was that they could not even approximately be compared to Saur's speech. Has he, as psychologists say, 'internalized' the role of sinner to such an extent that he now has to be corrected by the facts?)

===== In a telephone conversation, I pointed out to Speer that Giesler – as one is able to gather from his *Memoirs*

– disputes his claim that Hitler wanted his last resting place to be in the tower of the Party Forum in Linz. Speer was already familiar with the passage. 'Giesler is mistaken', he said, with a firmness in which one could detect something of the old resentment against his rival. Of course, he does not know why Hitler said nothing about it to Giesler. Perhaps it embarrassed him to let Giesler in on the matter. Giesler had been not only thoroughly alien to him but too narrow-minded to grasp such an unusual idea. But it cannot be completely ruled out that the defeated Hitler, the Hitler of the last years, let the idea drop.

===== Two weeks later. After a long break, Speer called again twice in the last few days. There is something 'careless', as he put it, which slipped out of him in a letter to an association of South African Jews. He handed the text of this, which already goes back a while, to an English journalist who was writing a portrait of him: the piece is due to appear in the *Sunday Times*, as well as in *Die Zeit* in Hamburg. The German translation was sent to him a few days ago for him to look over, and he read with dismay the conclusions that the journalist had drawn from his remark that the persecution of Jews in the Third Reich took place with his 'approval'.

Speer wants *Die Zeit* to insert a footnote in which he can explain that 'approval' does not signify 'knowledge' of the details. We then spoke about the distinction between 'knowing' and 'suspecting' that had apparently been a bone of contention in his interview with the journalist. 'Suspecting' comes more from allusions or rumours, and the very fact that there is a word for both indicates that there is a difference. I said to him that 'suspecting' precisely describes the (limited) state of knowledge of most Germans. As he claims of himself, they 'suspected' just enough to realize that it was better not to 'know'. Their behaviour was not completely purposeless in stopping at 'suspicions' and fearfully ensuring that they never learned the whole truth. Speer wants to give me the footnote (just one sentence) or to read it over the telephone, so that I can look it over before he sends it to the editors at *Die Zeit*.

The harmonious discussion got Speer talking. He spoke about recent trips he has made, about his family and the house in the Allgäu region that he acquired not long ago. Suddenly – I cannot remember the transition – we again came to the question of how much he had known. I repeated the sceptical objections that I have always presented to him.

After a long pause, he said that he had acted 'thoughtlessly' in his answer to the Board of Deputies. He hopes that the affair will end well, and I tried to calm him down. He added: 'You have to think so much about every utterance, and as you know I have always been a little careless in what I say.' As Hitler's minister, he soon broke the habit of carelessness, but in Spandau and after his release he fell back into the bad old ways. All that is now behind him, though, as it was in the old days. The difference is not so great, he said, with an ironic laugh. He must learn again how to weigh his words precisely. Sometimes he thought that, when you are at liberty, you are really free. Most people are, in fact. And then, with a little hesitation: 'But I'm not.'

===== Today, the vagaries of conversation first brought us to the offer made a while ago by a former leading employee at the Munich Party Archives of the NSDAP, Professor Priesack. One day Priesack told me that he is in possession of a few hundred documents, some of them private, which were salvaged at the end of the war. They consist mainly of instructions from Hitler or leading people in the Party, but also of 'politically and biographically exciting posthumous papers', including a letter confirming Hitler's knowledge and approval of Rudolf Hess's flight to Britain in the spring of 1941, and another document ordering the removal of Field-Marshal Erwin Rommel 'by one means or another'. Priesack later said that, among the most spectacular finds previously unknown to him, there are not only three volumes of Hitler's diaries with very personal details, but also around a dozen poems from the front that 'the unknown runner',[4] as he suddenly put it in the language of the times, composed during the First World War. The 'real sensation', though, is a nude portrait of Eva Braun by Hitler himself, 'the naked Frau Hitler', he added rather superfluously. He wants a total of 150,000 Deutschmarks[5] for the right to print the bundle of papers, and he would give preference for their reproduction in the *Frankfurter Allgemeine Zeitung*, possibly in a special supplement.

I went to Munich after several telephone conversations with Herr Priesack, and have now informed Speer so that he can examine the offer. Before I looked through the high piles of papers lying unsorted on Priesack's living-room table, I wanted to know where they had actually come from. After some humming and hawing, he replied that all he could say was that they were the highly personal materials which Hitler, in the days when the end was approaching, roughly a week before his suicide in the bunker, got out of Berlin in an aircraft that is thought to have later been brought down by a Russian shell near Börnersdorf in Saxony. The present owner, at that time a boy of sixteen evacuated to the countryside, hid and finally buried a number of containers from the debris of the aircraft. He has since made a successful career for himself and is 'a highly placed figure in the GDR government apparatus'. Professor Priesack insisted that this information was strictly confidential, since if any of it 'became known' the man would, for easily understandable reasons, be in the gravest danger. But he trusted me, especially as he had made enquiries about me in various quarters.

On this aspect, I told Speer, we had already had a difference of opinion that would be difficult to reconcile. If he had told me, I said to Priesack, that the 'supplier' lived among a tribe of cannibals somewhere at the heart of the Amazon jungle, he would have been easier for me to reach, and his credibility would have been easier to verify, than in the case of a man from the 'government apparatus of the GDR'. So, I could not help suspecting that the identity of the person in question had been all too cunningly concocted. Priesack replied that he could understand my doubts, but that a certain risk was attached to getting a 'world sensation' of this kind.

I informed Speer that I had then looked through some of the documents. My scepticism grew even stronger when I realized that I would not be able to see any of Hitler's three diaries, and that the nude picture of Eva Braun was available only as a photograph. Priesack could show me these items only when the negotiations were 'advancing' and were as good as concluded, and, if possible, the first remittance had been made.

In the end I suggested coming back with an expert who was very proud of his critical knowledge of the sources, and I mentioned the name of the Stuttgart historian Eberhard Jäckel. Priesack said he agreed. And when I subsequently told Jäckel of the offer, but also of doubts that kept growing the more I thought about it, he decided a little later to go and see Priesack and to take a close look at the documents.

Once again, however, there was no sign of the original diaries, the nude portrait or Hitler's dozen youthful poems, and when we got no further on the provenance of the material I decided to reject the offer. I thought it was so unserious that for a long time I said nothing about it either to a circle of friends well versed in contemporary history or, as I now informed him, to Speer. (*Addendum.* By the way, Eberhard Jäckel was in raptures over the sources and continued negotiating; he then acquired, for whatever payment, the publication rights for a large number of items in the hoard, including Hitler's supposed poems from the front. In 1980 he published these as part of a thick volume entitled: *Hitler. Sämtliche Aufzeichnungen 1905–1924.* This is still rightly considered a standard work, even though, soon after publication, Jäckel was obliged to hand in a list of corrections. For the sixty or more documents from the Priesack material turned out to be complete fakes.)

But that came later. When I told Speer about the negotiations with Priesack and his mountains of material, including the diaries, and when I explained that I had turned down the offer, he merely laughed. 'You did right!' he said. For Hitler had not been a man for diaries; the very idea seemed to him absurd. Still crazier, though, was the claim that Hitler had produced a nude picture of Eva Braun. The Führer could never have been talked into such an exposure of his beloved – assuming that he would have wanted to do it anyway. For both of them, Hitler and Eva Braun, were extremely prudish, as he can say from numerous observations, and everyone knew that Hitler would not let a doctor near him, not even Dr Morell. He had only one word for all that: 'Trickery!' And, as for the supposed poems, when he recently leafed through Jäckel's book he came across many lines that seemed very well known ('If one of us grows tired . . .').[6] As for Hitler's reaction to the report of his 'deputy' Rudolf Hess's flight to Britain, he had personally witnessed the scene. Hitler's rage kept erupting for days on end and even produced fits of choking. That could never have been play-acting! He had just kept repeating: 'Stupid little fake! Never anything genuine! Nothing! I can vouch for it!'

===== (*Addendum*. The sequel is well known. When the production of the supposed diaries had grown to sixty volumes, the material landed with *Stern* magazine. As soon as I heard that the editors were negotiating over them, I rang up and tried to warn my fellow journalists but was unsuccessful. By then they had evidently long ago made the decision 'to rewrite the history of the Hitler period'.)

===== May 1979. Speer on the phone today. For years he has been behaving exactly as the whole world demands of Germans: he is understanding, aware of his guilt, willing to engage in public repentance and self-incrimination; in short, he has been serious about 'coming to terms with the past', to the best of his ability and as far as such things are possible. The disappointing thing is that no one gives him credit for this, or anyway much too little. He does not suspect that this has to do with his lack of personal credibility. Rather, he thinks that the public at home and abroad has developed an image of the diehard Nazi that no soul-searching on his part can change. For numerous reasons, many may think it more useful to regard him and his generation as incorrigible evildoers.

Later. In Spandau he read the books of renegade communists such as Koestler, Gide and Silone. As far as he remembers, some of them explained that they had often heard of Stalin's crimes but had simply not believed it. 'Why', he asked, 'do people accept from them what no believes of me, and why on top of that are they even acclaimed as moral heroes?' And still later: 'There are evidently no diehard communists.'

===== March 1980. Siedler for two days in Kronberg. Speer heard of it and asked if we would mind if he came over for tea on his way through.

Discussion of one thing and another. To the question as to why he kept going back to the Maria Laach abbey, Speer replied with a trace of irony that perhaps nostalgia for the conditions in Spandau had something to do with it: the cells, the frugal meals, the strict rules for study. Anyway he finds at Maria Laach the inner peace that he misses everywhere else. He also mentioned a Father Athanasius with whom he had 'good discussions', just as he did before with the Spandau prison chaplain, Georges Casalis, whom he was glad to meet again recently.

Of course, he added, Maria Laach is a kind of escape; sometimes that is held against him, but the reproach does not bother him. He knows his way around when it comes to escapes, he said, not without ambiguity, and has long been an 'expert' in them. He also finds it increasingly difficult to listen to the many people who come to visit him in Heidelberg. Only with a great effort can he tolerate the curiosity and the lust for sensation that has driven them there, as if he were a freak in a deep cage, the calf with two heads, or anyway still the object of scrutiny that he felt himself to be in Spandau. But he does not want to turn down any requests for a visit. Besides, you can never predict whether a particular encounter will be rewarding. Some have been extremely worthwhile. Very few, on the whole, and 'they were nearly always unknown people about whom I had expected nothing at the beginning.'

══════ In the late evening, when Speer had been gone for some time, we talked again about his retreats to the abbey cell. I asked Siedler whether it had struck him too how clear the sky was above Speer. Whenever a metaphysical subject was as much as broached, he fell into an embarrassed and, if we persisted, almost tormented silence; he did not have the slightest thing to say about it. In any event, he has again and again given me the impression that the so-called last things are infinitely remote from him.

But, Siedler objected, why in his Spandau years did he read Karl Barth, Martin Buber, Albert Schweitzer and a dozen other theological writers, including Augustine and Thomas Aquinas, as he has mentioned on various occasions, and why has he always tried to have discussions with clergy-men? Why does he regularly withdraw to a monastery of all places? It may be, I suggested, that he hopes to get from books, discussions and the solitude of cells a few degrees of the human warmth that is denied him everywhere else.

That sounds reasonably illuminating, Siedler said. But there is still the question of why someone keeps knocking on doors that are closed to him. Speer is not made for such pointless behaviour. He must always have reasons and results, as I know just as well as he.

I replied that Speer, like many people, may like brooding for the sake of brooding and expects no answer from it. Finally, we again criticized some of Speer's character traits, and I asked whether the type of the well-meaning idealist, which for good or ill he largely embodies, ever knows what guilt is and how someone with his record in life should engage with his past. Can someone like Speer understand at all what he has perpetrated? Is he not, as it were, constitu-tionally incapable of it? So that he has nothing to deny or repress?

The same for anything like final questions. – And no answers.

10

THE UNANSWERED QUESTIONS

Early March 1981. On the journey from Basle to Frankfurt, as agreed not long ago, stopover in Heidelberg. Wonderful early spring day. Speer not in such a good mood for a long time, almost happy (strangely inappropriate word for him!) about our first meeting for more than a year. General impression that the burden is gradually lifting from him – perhaps, I involuntarily thought, he still has a couple of reasonably 'normal' years ahead of him. He said that visitors are no longer coming in such countless numbers as a while ago, and he attempted a pun with *Last* [burden] and *Lästigkeit* [nuisance] that he could not really handle. Anyway, after the turbulent years he has patiently lived through, something new: the 'happiness of being forgotten'.

Walk after lunch down the Schloss-Wolfsbrunnenweg to the Neckar, then back up with long detours. Discussion of a lot of incidental things. But for the first time I had the feeling that Speer is coping with life without a task. A little surprisingly to myself, I suddenly plucked up some courage and returned with rather elaborate caution to what he had known of the crimes. What interests me, I began, is not the tiresome 'reporter's questions' (as he called them) about his guilt; all that is long behind us. I was simply looking for an explanation for myself and did not expect any confessions.

As he knew, I doubted for factual reasons that he had been ignorant during those years (leaving aside the obscure reference to Auschwitz by the Breslau gauleiter Hanke). I did not want to put his honesty in question; he had proven it during the many years of our work together, most recently in relation to the speech by Saur, when he had made no small impression on me. But we both knew how unlimited was the human power to suppress things, and perhaps we were a little closer to tracking down the mechanism at work there.

He listened attentively, with a concerned expression, while I made every effort to avoid an interrogatory tone. Was it not the case, I continued, that at Nuremberg he had initially had no choice but to deny knowledge of the atrocities: not only because he, if only for what he called 'sporting' reasons, had wanted to win the battle for his life, but also because he had needed to preserve a modicum of self-respect? It was not hard to imagine the shock he felt, given his middle-class background and so on, to find himself in the dock with mass murderers such as Kaltenbrunner or Frank and characters like Streicher. He would understandably have wanted to distance himself from them, this time not only because it corresponded to his inclinations but also for the sake of, as it were, his spiritual survival.

When he was released from Spandau twenty years later, I continued, questions concerning his knowledge of the crimes were again raised at the first press conference in Hotel Gerhus. And it was perfectly understandable to me that in such a situation he maintained, had to maintain, his Nuremberg line. Certainly he would have lost all credibility

if he had then retracted his challenge to the prosecution at
Nuremberg and, for example, declared that it had been
merely a tactical instrument for his defence. One can easily
picture that this would have cast him as a real Nazi villain:
first debasing himself as a common accomplice of criminals,
then putting on a show of pained innocence, and finally,
when he could no longer be prosecuted, triumphantly telling
the world of his lies.

When we had climbed back to his house from the Neckar,
I added that one would not even have to take into account
the self-righteousness of the opinion-formers to realize how
impossible he would have made things for himself by taking
such a course. In any event, it was clear to me that he had
had no choice but to continue disputing the case against him.
By that time, moreover, his knowledge (which, even in my
view, had been rather fragmentary) would obviously have
faded in his memory. Then I asked whether he could say that
it had been roughly like that. For me, at least, such an
account would clear up some of the mystery of his 'evasive
performances'. Probably for many others too.

Speer came to a halt. He suddenly seemed tired and again
had the melancholy look he always displayed when the discussion came to that subject. 'My dear Herr Fest', he said,
touching with a rare gesture the familiarity of my arm, 'you
should not keep asking me such unanswerable questions.'
Then, by moving a couple of steps ahead, he showed that he
intended to say no more.

Was this a 'confession'? I wondered later, on my return
journey. In substance it probably was. But he had visibly kept
open a little escape route.

====== When we reached his house at the end of our walk,
however, he indirectly came back to the subject once more.
He had always expected, he said, that everything would be

Albert Speer, 1980

easier for him after the years of imprisonment. In the end he had admitted his responsibility, confessed his guilt, served his allotted sentence and even endured complete isolation. But he had been deceiving himself, and perhaps never as much as on this matter.

For he had not rid himself of any of the burden, he said in conclusion, as if he wanted this to be really the last word on the matter and to provide me with a certain satisfaction. Even I had kept reminding him of it, he said. Of course, my reasons were different from those of most, and he respected that. But sometimes it seemed to him that there had been no point in all that thinking, all that tenacious effort. It had probably all been futile, like most of what he had undertaken in life. He had long ceased to look for an answer. He knew of none. And, when we arrived in front of the house after walking silently for a long time beside each other, again: 'Do you perhaps?'

===== A call from Speer. The *Memoirs* are going to be filmed by an American production company. There had been talk of it several times before, but now the project seems to have taken shape. Speer said that the *Spandau Diaries* evidently gave them an idea of how his life could be translated. Apparently a second (German?) company is also interested. Everything he says about it sounds a little confused, so one wonders whether it will really come to pass. He wanted to know if, by any chance, I would be willing to collaborate in some way. I declined, however, by referring to my numerous duties.

===== Speer on the telephone. For only the second time in all these years, he speaks spontaneously and in detail about the architect Rudolf Wolters. True, his name has come up now and then as helper, family friend, account administrator, and other things besides. But, because of his shyness about anything to do with feelings, Speer always left the subject out and was so taciturn in response to any enquiry that we never pushed him further. Nor does the name appear in his manuscripts – or, if it does, only in an unimportant context.

Only once, many years ago, did Speer refer to Wolters in discussion as the closest friend he had. And he added that, during the Spandau years, Wolters performed invaluable services for him; he does not know how or whether he would have survived those years without Wolters's support. Then Speer spoke of the 'boundless admiration' that Wolters had shown him. He added in a tone of amusement that, back in the early 1940s, his friend had compared him in a paper to Palladio, Brunelleschi and even Leonardo and named him as Schinkel's legitimate successor: 'Well, we did both love grand comparisons!'

Speer described Wolters as a thoroughly independent mind, self-confident and with a tendency to irony that protected him from all the devout faith required in those years. With Speer's help he had even been able to avoid joining the Party. Wolters is not at all prepared to defend the regime on principle, nor, as he (Speer) has seen on many occasions, to become the 'posthumous Nazi' in the face of sweeping condemnations on all sides.

But there were also differences of opinion between them during the Spandau years. Wolters reproached him in a friendly way for taking much too sharp a distance from the Hitler period: not from the ideology (which he too thought crazy) but from the enthusiasm that had overwhelmed and inspired them, especially in their planning activity, or from their intense emotions and, of course, their mistakes. Speer used to say in those days that, however bitter it was, he had to accept that life sometimes separated even friends. He did not want to mention Wolters in the *Memoirs*, since, 'given the state of things at the time', it could not be ruled out that he would feel offended by any reference to his name. We made no attempt to make Speer change his mind. He seemed understanding and unhappy.

Today, no understanding was in evidence. Speer was indignant and spoke of 'betrayal'. Wolters had dealt him a 'stab in the back' and disclosed the most confidential matters to a young doctoral student – in particular, certain unauthorized manoeuvres that Wolters conducted during the prison years in relation to the 'chronicle' that had been kept by Speer's department. Unforgivably, Wolters had not actually claimed but given the impression that the cuts in the original text were made on Speer's initiative. In reality, he had had nothing to do with them and only subsequently condoned the interference in order to spare his friend.

When I wanted to know what the deleted passages had contained, Speer evaded the issue. 'Nothing but trivia', he said – but this only encouraged the idea that he had been an accomplice in the falsification of a document. On being asked why he had never mentioned it to us, he fell into a long silence until I asked whether he was still on the line. He answered my repeated request for details with what I called his 'ministerial voice': the matter was closed a long time ago, and anyway nothing could be changed after the publication of the books of recollections. Then he said he would not put up with it, and spoke of the lawyers he would call in.

I registered numerous doubts. In particular, I said that quarrels between friends can never be settled by legal argument. Whoever you are, you inevitably cut a nasty figure by taking that route. He again fell silent for a long time, then replied that he would think it over. When I made another attempt to find out something about the excisions in the text, he simply said: 'Let's drop it!'

———— It looks as if Speer did consult lawyers in the end. In any case, Siedler reported an announcement in today's *Börsenblatt* that is clearly directed against Wolters. 'An almighty stupidity', Siedler said, 'which will expose him in the eyes of the world. What the devil got into him!' I told him of our conversation and said that I had tried to talk Speer out of doing it. He had spoken to Siedler, too, who also strongly advised against it. But Siedler knows no more than I do about the cuts that Wolters made in the chronicle.

===== Late March 1981. Speer in Frankfurt. He invited me to a meal. Not a word about yesterday's friend; everything I tried fell on deaf ears. Instead, not without a certain satisfaction, Speer spoke about the fact that he had 'coped with his third life reasonably successfully' and, against all probability, brought it to a defensible conclusion. Was he saying that to encourage himself? I wondered. In any case, his words seemed louder than usual.

His new book, *Der Sklavenstaat*, is more or less finished, and although, on thematic grounds, it cannot be compared to the two others, he is convinced that it provides important insights. A lot of what he came across during his work at the archives horrified and alarmed him. He was disappointed and confused when I again told him that I could not take on any kind of final editing. From then on he was monosyllabic. But I never gave him reason to expect anything like that.

Then about the announcement in the *Börsenblatt*. I said I hoped that everything would not collapse if Wolters launched a campaign against him. 'What would collapse?' Speer asked with a polite change of tone, and for a moment the old mistrust seemed to be there again. But I was wrong. A little later, Speer said that he was falling between two stools. Some tormented him with routine questions, while others got out of his way, and still others, like Wolters, declared their contempt and even open hostility towards him.

At the end, Speer said he was well aware that, if he were to relent and make some casual concession, it would help him out of this perpetual dilemma and win back a large part of his former companions. When I reacted with silent astonishment, he said with an imperceptible smile: 'Don't worry! Those few words would certainly make my life more bearable. But you'll never hear them from me. For the first time I now have firm convictions.'

Does he really? I asked myself after we had said goodbye. Far more does one feel how much his loneliness troubles him.

===== Mid-April. Siedler told of some past visits of Speer's to Berlin, when he had had to tell him once more that he did not want to publish *Der Sklavenstaat*, especially as I would have no time to take on the editing. (I had received three or four chapters of the rough draft to look over, but they looked very messy and in need of a lot of work.)

During one of these discussions, Siedler said, Speer began to speak with the embarrassment of a 'schoolboy', about a 'great love' and his relationship with a young woman living as a German in England; she was married there and had two children, but felt isolated in a cold and prejudiced environment. He eventually brought along a photo, which showed him and the attractive woman looking cheerful and light-hearted on a hotel balcony in Provence. Siedler was rather taken aback, not least because of Speer's statement that he had had to pass sixty before experiencing his first intense erotic relationship.

I said that Speer had obviously found in this woman the one who freed him from his past and brought him back to the present; who did not burden him with constant questions and find his answers unsatisfactory. It was hard for me to begrudge him it, however much sympathy I also had for his wife in Heidelberg.

===== 1 September 1981. Speer died unexpectedly this afternoon in a London hotel. Attempts to reach his friend

Norman Stone, who had done an interview with Speer in the morning for the BBC and was probably with him until midday. No success. Probably rushing between TV and radio stations as the last witness.

===== October 1981. A lot of advance talk about the book by one Dr Matthias Schmidt, who tears 'the mask from Speer's face'. Wolters's foreman, then. One can only hope that, as Speer claimed, the promised evidence concerns only 'trivia'. Siedler behaves as if he is convinced of it, but he admits to not yet having read the text.

===== Read M. Schmidt's book. Very biased, but the evidence not actually inconsiderable. Altogether it contains exactly what I sometimes feared: contrary to Speer's assertions, there are some 'secrets'. Disappointed and annoyed. I said to Siedler today that Speer, with the most innocent face in the world, led us all up the garden path. I am not prepared to let him get away with it. And, as 'fate's favourite child', which is how he saw himself all his life, it is fitting that he left the stage – or rather, was carried from the stage – just before the exposure took place.

Undeserved good fortune. Anyway, he has been spared having to say anything about it. We occasionally called him 'everybody's darling'. That obviously does not apply only to other people. Fortune also looked on him as a kind of 'darling'. Possibly more than he was entitled to.

===== Two days later. On the telephone again with Siedler. He feels that my 'condemnation', as he calls it, is too harsh and somewhat disrespectful. A later judgement would have to take all sides into consideration.

One can scarcely contradict him. But why did Speer want to make me believe that Wolters had briefed Schmidt only about the falsification business, without mentioning the more important matter to which it related: the evacuation operation in Berlin? I said that Speer's behaviour was inexcusable and recalled that he had once told us of the first lesson he learned, in his student years or even earlier: namely, that in practical life one has to cope with contradictions. He has now supplied us with another example of this. Unfortunately I am not sure it is the last.

═════ (*A supplementary remark, some ten years later*. A few days ago Albert Speer Junior rang to ask whether I could come to Frankfurt for a meal with Gitta Sereny. As I knew, she was working on a biography of his father and wanted to obtain some information from him. But he had reasons to have the discussion with her only in the presence of a third person. When I asked what that meant, he replied that he had had certain 'differences' after talking with his father and other members of the family, and he wanted to avoid any 'troubles' of that kind.

I had met Frau Sereny now and then and occasionally mentioned her name to Speer himself. I therefore agreed to the request, though not without advising him to inform Frau Sereny in advance, if at all possible, about my participation in the meeting. Speer Junior said he would try to do that.

When I arrived at midday yesterday in the lobby of the Frankfurter Hof hotel, Frau Sereny was already there. Seeing me looking at her, she immediately flared up and asked whether I had come on her account. When I said 'yes', she hit the roof and barked at me: 'Clear off! I didn't ask you to come. You're bothering me! I want to speak with Albert, not you. You have no business being here!' She dismissed my reply that I was simply following Herr Speer's wishes and continued her torrent of words: 'Go away! I don't want you around!' and so on. My proposal to let Herr Speer decide was swallowed up by her agitation. Albert had nothing to decide, she said, again using the familiar first name. It was she who had asked for the meeting, and she would have said if she had wanted to have a witness there.

Albert Speer appeared and insisted that he would speak to her only in the presence of an independent and trustworthy third person. She uttered something offensively mistrustful and said that she conducted all her interviews in private with the interviewee alone, whoever he or she might be. To calm her down, Herr Speer suggested going to have a meal. She reluctantly gave way, but let it be known that she no longer saw any point in the meeting and that all the time had been wasted. In fact, the table talk was quite an effort throughout: not a word was said about Speer Senior, and as soon as we had drunk coffee Frau Sereny abruptly stood up and swept away with an aggrieved air.

If she had known, she would perhaps have thought about the fact that I had the above notes in my briefcase all the time, and that I had wanted to give them to her for her work. Attached to them was a little note in which I said that she could do with them what she wished, treat Speer's testimony as reliable or unreliable, but that anyway she might find them useful, if only to compare what Speer had said with her own notes. I myself, I added, had no use for these notes and was contemplating handing them over to an archive, such as that of the Institute for Contemporary History.

Gitta Sereny's remarkable entrance foiled this plan. When her book on Speer came out a few years later, I re-read the preceding notes and soon reversed my decision not to write the story of Albert Speer's life. The biography was published in 1999.)

CHRONOLOGY

19 March 1905	Albert Speer born into an upper-middle-class family in Mannheim. His parents: Albert Friedrich Speer, architect, and Luise Mathilde Speer.
1923	Begins to study architecture in Karlsruhe.
1924	Transfers to the Technische Hochschule in Munich.
1925	Continues his studies in Berlin, where he meets his teacher Heinrich Tessenow.
1928	After his diploma examination, becomes a university lecturer.
28 August 1928	Marries Margret Weber.
Late 1930	At a meeting place in the Hasenheide in Berlin, Speer hears a speech by Adolf Hitler for the first time. He is deeply impressed by Hitler's

	personality and his vision of Germany's future.
January 1931	Joins the NSDAP (membership no. 474481) and the Sturmabteilung (SA). Sets up on his own as an architect in Mannheim.
1932	Receives his first building contract from the NSDAP.
30 January 1933	Adolf Hitler appointed Chancellor of the Reich.
March 1933	Speer contracted by Joseph Goebbels to rebuild the Propaganda Ministry. For necessary work on the Reich Chancellery, Hitler thereupon names Speer as assistant to his favourite Munich architect, Paul Ludwig Troost.
January 1934	After Troost's surprising death, Speer becomes Hitler's most important architect. In the following period, he designs a large number of emblematic monumental buildings. In the German Labour Front (DAF), he heads the 'Beauty of Labour' department. Responsible for urban construction at Rudolf Hess's General Staff.
1934–7	At the World Exhibition in Paris, Speer receives the 'Grand Prix' for his work in designing the all-German Party Conference Centre in Nuremberg and the Gold Medal for the German Pavilion in Paris. Hitler appoints him General Building

	Inspector for the reshaping of Berlin and other German cities.
1938	Appointment of Speer to the Prussian State Council. Decorated with the Golden Party Badge of the NSDAP.
8–9 November 1938	*Reichskristallnacht*: Nazi-organized pogrom against the Jews.
1938–9	Speer develops a general plan for the reconstruction of Berlin as World Capital 'Germania'. Builds the New Reich Chancellery on Voss-Strasse and designs models for many other monumental buildings and Nazi cult centres. Hitler gives him unlimited financial scope.
1 September 1939	German invasion of Poland and beginning of Second World War. Speer becomes increasingly preoccupied with military construction, for which he builds up his own organization, the 'Speer Building Staff'.
1941	Becomes Reichstag representative for Berlin West.
1941–2	After the German invasion of the Soviet Union, armaments minister Fritz Todt charges Speer with the reconstruction of factories and the railway network in Ukraine.
8 February 1942	Speer becomes Reich Minister for Weapons and Munitions, as successor to Fritz Todt, who died earlier that day in an accident. Despite damage to German infrastructure

and raw materials supply from Allied bombing raids, he is able to keep raising arms production. It reaches its peak in autumn 1944.

2 September 1943 — Grouping of Speer's various administrative apparatuses in the Reich Ministry for Armaments and War Production.

6 October 1943 — Conference in Poznań at which Heinrich Himmler gives his notorious speech.

Early 1944 — Speer is seriously ill and cannot do his job after the new year. The growing shortage of raw materials and manpower threatens collapse of the war economy. Although Speer argues for an end to the war, Hitler persuades him to remain in office.

July 1944 — After the failed attempt on Hitler's life on 20 July, resistance documents come to light in which Speer is named as minister in a new government. But he is able to make it appear credible that he was not informed of these and had no conspiratorial contact with those behind the putsch.

1944–5 — Speer opposes Hitler's 'scorched earth' policy. He sabotages orders intended to destroy Germany's transport system and entire infrastructure, as well as industry and agriculture.

23–4 April 1945 — Speer's farewell visit to Hitler in the bunker of the Reich Chancellery in Berlin.

30 April 1945	Suicides of Adolf Hitler and Eva Braun.
7–8 May 1945	Unconditional surrender of Germany.
23 May 1945	Speer arrested at Schloss Glücksburg. Transferred to the Allied military prison in Nuremberg.
20 November 1945	Opening of International Military Tribunal in Nuremberg, to try leading figures of the Third Reich, including Hermann Goering, Joachim von Ribbentrop, Rudolf Hess and Albert Speer. Speer is the only defendant who admits his complete responsibility and guilt for the crimes of the regime.
1 October 1946	Speer sentenced to twenty years' imprisonment by the Nuremberg Tribunal and incarcerated in Spandau prison, Berlin. Many appeals for mercy by Speer's family and various politicians fail because of Soviet objections.
30 September 1966	Release from Spandau prison.
1969	The *Memoirs* are published by Propyläen Verlag in Berlin and become a worldwide bestseller.
1975	The *Spandau Diaries* published in Frankfurt, Berlin and Vienna.
1981	*Der Sklavenstaat. Meine Auseinandersetzungen mit der SS* published in Stuttgart. (English translation: *The Slave State: Heinrich Himmler's Masterplan for SS Supremacy*, trans.

Joachim Neugroschel, London: Weidenfeld & Nicolson, 1981.)

1 September 1981   Albert Speer dies in a London clinic during a trip to England.

TRANSLATOR'S NOTES

Introduction

1 Joachim C. Fest, *The Face of the Third Reich*, trans. Michael Bullock, London: Weidenfeld & Nicolson, 1970.

2 Albert Speer, *Spandau: The Secret Diaries*, trans. Richard and Clara Winston, London: Weidenfeld & Nicolson, 1976.

3 Joachim Fest, *Speer: The Final Verdict*, trans. Ewald Osers and Alexandra Dring, London: Weidenfeld & Nicolson, 2001.

Chapter 1 Drawing Closer

1 One of the imprints of Ullstein Publishers.

2 Literally, wandering or migratory bird: a member of the Wandervogel ramblers' association, founded in 1895, one of the constituents of what came to be known as the German Youth Movement.

3 In English in the original.

4 The central Berlin park in which Hitler gave the speech in 1930 that is mentioned in the introduction.

5 Following his abortive putsch in November 1923, Hitler was sentenced to five years' imprisonment in the Landsberg fortress west of Munich; he eventually served just eight months.

Chapter 2 In the Innermost Circle

1 Hitler's famed residence in the Obersalzberg.

2 Wilhelm Brückner: Hitler's chief adjutant until 1940, later a Wehrmacht colonel. Theodor Morell: Hitler's personal physician from 1936 until his suicide in 1945. Julius Schaub: Hitler's chief adjutant after the sacking of Brückner in 1940.

3 The conference of Nazi officials and gauleiters held at Posen, eastern Germany (now Poznań, Poland), at which Speer gave a speech on the morning of 6 October 1943.

4 Mainz was in the zone of Germany occupied by the French from 1919 until 1930.

5 Cola di Rienzi: the medieval Italian populist who, having crushed a nobles' rebellion, found the tide of popular opinion turning against him and died making a last stand in the Capitol. Wagner's eponymous opera, which Hitler saw as a young man in Linz, is based on Bulwer-Lytton's novel *Rienzi: The Last of the Tribunes*.

6 That is: the Flying Dutchman, hero of Wagner's opera.

7 Hanns Johst (1890–1978): novelist, playwright and Nazi Party functionary, whose play *Der König* dates from 1920.

8 Winifred Wagner (1897–1980): daughter-in-law of Richard Wagner and, after the death of her husband Siegfried in 1930, director of the Bayreuth festival.

9 Hitler's friend and official photographer, who had joined the Nazi Party in 1920.

10 In 1935 Strauss was forced to resign as president of the Reichsmusikkammer, after he had refused to remove the name of Stefan Zweig from the notice for his *Die schweigsame Frau* (on which Zweig had worked as librettist).

11 A 'lift', in the sense of a shared ride in a car.

12 A style of theatre, exemplified by Goebbels's own *Der Wanderer*, which harked back to a Germanic past shrouded in myth. It knew a brief vogue between 1931 and 1937.

Chapter 3 *Highs and Lows*

1 The reference is to the battle fought in AD 553 near Mount Vesuvius, where the Ostrogoths were defeated by the generals of the Eastern Roman Empire and driven from Italy.

2 Speer's theory, endorsed by Hitler, that the eventual collapse of a building should leave behind ruins of aesthetic value testifying to the grandeur of the civilization that produced them.

3 Karl Friedrich Schinkel (1781–1841): the Romantic-Classical architect and city planner of the Prussian state, at work in Berlin after 1815.

4 Hitler's order of 19 March 1945 prescribing a 'scorched earth' policy in the face of the advancing Allied armies.

Chapter 4 *The Minister*

1 The low-lying coastal strip of land lying inshore of the North and East Frisian islands.

Chapter 5 *Breaking with Hitler*

1 The date of the failed attempt on Hitler's life.

2 Heinz Guderian (1888–1954): acting chief of staff after the July attempt on Hitler's life.

Chapter 6 Completion of the Memoirs
1 The art historian and director of the Dresden Art Gallery.
2 Johannes Gross (1932–1999): well-known German journalist and political commentator.
3 Gitta Sereny, *Albert Speer: His Battle with Truth*, London: Macmillan, 1995.

Chapter 7 On the End and the Farewell to Hitler
1 The reference is to the famous telegram that Goering sent from Berchtesgaden, offering to take over command of the Reich as Hitler's designated successor.
2 East–west axis: Speer's (unfinished) project for an ornate thirty-mile route across Berlin.
3 The Fieseler Fi 156 Storch was an observation monoplane used by the German armed forces throughout the Second World War.

Chapter 8 Trial, Prison Years, Release
1 As the text suggests, the German quotation is not altogether accurate. See the English translation by Marianne Cowan, which closely follows the original German: 'If you gaze long into an abyss, the abyss will gaze back into you.' Friedrich Nietzsche, *Beyond Good and Evil* (section 146), Chicago: Gateway, 1955, p. 85.

Chapter 9 Expert in Escapes
1 Literally, 'revulsion for knowledge'.
2 'Durch Berechnung unwissend'. The allusion is to Amfortas's description of the holy fool as 'durch Mitleid wissend' (enlightened through compassion), in Act I of Wagner's *Parsifal*.
3 Karl-Otto Saur (1902–1966): after Todt's death, permanent secretary and one of Speer's two de facto deputies in the armaments ministry.

4 Hitler enlisted in the German Army during the First World War and was given the job of dispatch runner.
5 Approximately US$100,000 at today's notional rate of exchange.
6 From the folk song 'Kameradschaft', composed in 1944 by Herybert Menzel, whose verse was often used by the Nazis for propaganda purposes.

INDEX

Note: page numbers in **bold** refer to illustrations; the initials 'AS' refer to Albert Speer